KELLY K

RECKLESS REVOLUTION

Revolution involves many but always starts with one

KELLY K

RECKLESS
REVOLUTION
LOVE

Revolution involves many but always starts with one

Reckless Love Revolution

Copyright © 2018 by Kelly K. Ministries All rights reserved

Published by Kelly K Ministries
PO Box 1112 Kingfisher OK 73750

Front cover design by Ian Lundin
www.CXXIIapparel.com

www.KellyKMinistries.com

ISBN: 9798397390989

NOTE TO THE READER

This book was originally released in 2018. The website mentioned and "WHY" cards are no longer available. And for that I am very sorry. However, the principle of "Reckless Love" hasn't changed at all. You don't need anything you don't already have to go out and love people to Jesus! And I pray that's exactly what this book will inspire you to do! Even as I read this book again after writing it 5 years ago, I am more excited than I have ever been to go love people and let them see what Jesus REALLY looks like. Now, go see what Jesus can do through YOU!

- Kelly K

Table of Contents

FORWARD

The reckless love of God is something our finite minds have a hard time trying to grasp. I suppose this is because we have been moulded by a culture that is built upon "getting" at any cost. From a young age we are told we need to win, to get ahead, to establish ourselves, build up our own supplies, and then maybe we will have something left over to give to others.

But the reckless love of God has none of these characteristics. It has no concern of it's own welfare, reputation or resources. It continues to give in the face of rejection, it pours out relentlessly, it is selfless, it honors, lifts up, builds and protects. The reckless love of God is everything we are not and all that Jesus is.

This is the great mystery of the Christian life - that God calls us; the broken, flawed and fickle vessels of this world to be the very conduit of this reckless love. How can it be that a perfect God would want to pour out a perfect love through us? The answer, through His perfect Son.

The truth is that God's love and whether God can love through us, is not dependent on us at all, it is totally dependent on Jesus. He makes us worthy, whether we feel like we are or not. His love remains faithful even when we are unfaithful. That is the amazing thing about it. It truly is reckless. It goes 'all in' without any promise of reward. It's risks doing the deal, despite the odds of it working out look so low, it recklessly loves anyway.

To be an outpost of God's reckless love is the call for every Christ follower on the earth today. This may sound like a huge and daunting task, but as you read the pages of this book, I am convinced that God's love will compel you to this great and holy task.

As for Kelly, I have served alongside of him as a fellow minister and I am honored to call him my friend. Every story you read in these pages shines a light, not on his own efforts, but completely on Jesus' work through him. Every word that is written is penned with truth and conviction. He challenges us from a place of humility and love. This man lives the message that he preaches. And the stories you read on these pages are only a snapshot of the love he shows in real life. He is a living example of the transformative, powerful and supernatural nature of the Reckless Love of God.

My prayer is that you would open your heart to that same power to work in and through you. That this would be a catalyst for you to love recklessly, love unashamedly and love with every part of your being - I guarantee you, it will be your greatest adventure yet.

-Jessica Clayton O'Dea
VERSES

ENDORSEMENTS

I had the privilege of meeting Kelly K in Cabo while vacationing with our wives, and became instant friends. He speaks the truth with a boldness and love that's hard to come by!!! He's a family man with a heart of gold. And I'm glad to call him a friend.

-Heath Miller

aka WWE Super Star Heath Slater

Kelly K has a heart to see lives changed. Not many put their money where their mouth is when it comes reaching the forgotten. I can tell Reckless Love is more than a name for him. He's really out in the streets fearlessly loving on people and motivating the next generation to do the same.

-Shonlock

Christian Hip-Hop Artist

My friend Kelly Kopp has written a book that will be a Call to Action' for everyone to love like Jesus did, with reckless abandon. Kelly walks you through the Bible and takes some of our favorite stories to show us how Jesus committed daily acts of Reckless Love and shows us how we can see and love like Jesus did. I could not put the book down and read it in one sitting. I believe you will too.

-Amor Sierra

Owner Miami Tattoo Company, Anti-human trafficking Advocate.

ACKNOWLEDGMENTS

Lindsay Kopp - You are my world! Thank you for listening to hundreds of my horrible, crazy, ideas over the years and always helping me go the right way. Thank you for supporting me and helping me pursue my passions and always pushing me forward, even when the road ahead looked impossible. Thank you for being the greatest mother I've ever seen, the best wife I could ever ask for, and for being the best friend I've ever had in the world. I absolutely love you forever!

Brennen, Chase, Avery, and Jaxx - The four of you have changed my life more than you can ever know. This book is for all of you more than it is for anyone else. If the four of you can get ahold of this Reckless Love of Jesus then my life will have made all the impact it's needed to make. You guys make me want to be a better person and go deeper with God daily. Thank you for being the best kids in the world! I love you so very much.

Dad - Thank you for the hours of talks we shared after school, football practice, and church. I will forever cherish your words of wisdom and I will pass them on to my kids as well. (And anyone else's kids who I can get to listen too!) Those talks shaped me into the man I am today and I'm so grateful to have a father that cared enough about me to teach me what REALLY matters in this life.
Thank you. I love you.

Mom (Echo) - I have a respect and love for you that I share with no one else on this earth! Of every person in my life, you're the only one who made the CHOICE to love me when you didn't have to, and at times, probably didn't even want to. You sacrificed so much in your own life for me. You have been the truest, greatest example of the Reckless Love of Jesus in my life. I can honestly say, without you, this book wouldn't exist. Loving people like Jesus is second nature to me because you never let me see that any other way was actually an option. Thank you for loving me recklessly. I'll be sure to pass it on to the rest of the world, God willing! I love you!

Mom (Karen) - I love you so much! As far back as I can remember, you've been the best audience in the world! You always laugh at my dumb jokes, you always fall for my pranks, and just being in the same room with you has always had a magical way of making my days better. We have never had the traditional mother/son relationship, but you've always been my favorite person to try and make smile! You also helped teach me what the Reckless Love of Jesus looked like as well, but in a totally different way! Without both perspectives this book would be shallow and one sided. Thank you. I love you. Can I cook this turkey in the microwave?

Andi & Brent - Where do I even begin to thank the two of you!
I literally would have given up on ministry by month two if it hadn't been for you guys! When things looked impossible, you always show up and help knock down walls. You are such a great example of Reckless Love that I aspire to reach your level. Thank you for believing in me and this vision no matter what challenges were standing in the way. I look up to you both so much and I'm honored God put you in my life to be such great examples! No matter where I am, I will always have a seat saved on the front row for both of you!

Mema & Papa - If I had to pick out my favorite people on earth, it would be the two of you! You're more like parents than grand-parents, but without the, "no cookies at bedtime rule". Thank you for always pouring love into me, forgiving me, and encouraging me. The reason our family is so blessed is because the two of you have always made the choice to put God first in all that you do and that practice has spread to the rest of us. Thank you for always being obedient to God and leading us all in the way He wanted us to go. I will always have time to sit and talk with you Mema, and go motorcycle riding with you, Papa. I love you both more than I could ever say with words. Thank you, thank you, thank you!

Pastor Randy - You're my best friend, mentor, and spiritual father. To say I could have done this without you would just be ridiculous! God knew I needed you in my life and I'm so thankful you stuck it out with me for the last twenty years! I love you brother,
YOU LOOK RESTED!

Kingdom Youth Conference Crew - Thank you, thank you, thank you! Thank you for taking a step in faith and letting an unknown, big, crazy, pierced, tattooed, Oklahomie, have a spot on your conference! I'll never forget the first day we all met, and how all of you looked at me like, "What have we done!?" But after that first weekend together we were family! I'm excited and blessed I get to do life with all of you. Let's keep going for a million more years!

Ryan Hinckley - I SAVED you for last... I didn't forget until last, I promise! There are not enough pages in this book for me to properly thank you for all you've done. God gives us the best gifts, and you were definitely a gift from God to my life! You're more than a friend, you're my brother. I'm privileged to GET to travel the world with you! You force me to be a better Christian just by living your life in such a Godly way that I want to be more like you. Thank you for always being selfless. I always see how you put me first over yourself in all we do. I may never tell you enough, but I want you to know that I see all you do, and I'm so eternally grateful. I couldn't do all I do if I didn't have you by my side. Let's keep going man, we're not even CLOSE to done!

INTRODUCTION
"Love, Crash, Heal"
- Soular

I woke up sliding down I-40 in Nashville Tennessee, on my back at seventy miles an hour. My body felt like I was on fire from head to toe. I didn't know if I was about to die, if I was already dead, or if this was all a horrible nightmare.

From a pattern of bad choices that had led me so far away from my original purpose of following God, I was at the end of a long and painful road and my heavenly Father was going to great lengths to get my attention. I didn't die that day, but there were times the pain was enough to make me wish it.

For the next three months, my life was a living nightmare, in and out of a burn center, undergoing the most excruciatingly painful procedures that I wouldn't wish on my worst enemy. But it was all worth it.

This event was responsible for a change in my direction. Without it, I'd likely still be following my own plan for fame and fortune. But God had a plan for me, He hadn't forgotten. No matter how hard I'd tried to prove my own worthlessness, disqualify myself, and destroy what He had planted in me, God still wanted to use me. God loves me.

The same goes for you.

By the time you finish this book, if you don't already know that these statements apply to you, you will. If I could wish one take away for you, from reading this book, it's this; until you understand God's love for you, you can never fully love others. This perfect love is so pure and comes with zero strings attached. When we finally get it, our only response can be,

 "I have to give this love to as many people as I possibly can."

Trust me on this, loving others and expecting nothing in return is the purest high you'll ever find in this life. It's more addicting than any drug, more fulfilling than any fame, and more fun than you've ever experienced.

Hopefully, you're not as stubborn as I was. I hope and pray that none of you will have to go through a horrific, life altering crash to begin your journey. In fact, you can choose to start it right now, here, today, and I hope my story can give you the inspiration you need to take the first step.

CHAPTER 1
"All You Need Is Love"
- The Beatles

It was Christmas 1997, and all I'd been asking for was this sweet Raiders Starter jacket. If you grew up in the 90's you're picturing this bad boy right now! I really didn't want anything else, and I just knew, that against all the odds I was going to get it.

So, One of the two wonderful women I have the pleasure of calling mom, Echo Kopp, is a beautiful soul that was born giving. Whether it be the shoes off her feet, or the shirt off MY back, if she saw someone in need and had the power to meet it, she felt compelled to do something. It wasn't out of pity, or pride of position, but genuine compassion and the understanding that she was only able to love others because someone had first loved her with a reckless abandon she knew she could never match. This is important information in moving forward with this story.

So, Echo hands me the gift, with a look of expectancy and I'm thinking, this is it. I unwrap it, mentally rehearsing my surprise. I didn't need to bother practicing shock, though, because, to my horror, instead of the gorgeous black and silver motif I'd been envisioning for months and drooling over on store racks, every time I saw one, there sat an abomination of a starter pullover with an Eagle's logo on it.

It was a nice jacket, don't get me wrong, and she'd obviously worked hard to get what I wanted. I could see she was proud of herself, so I swallowed my pride and accepted it. It had been on sale, and the savings, I'm sure, had gone to a good cause. But, it just wasn't the same. Out of love for my mom, I wore it anyway, without complaint. For a year.

As the months went by, I kept my eye out for that Raiders starter jacket, and a year later, she walked into the house with a big smile. There, was my pullover. She'd noticed how gratefully I accepted the substitution and was determined to find one at a price she felt she could afford. I was beyond happy. It was everything I could have hoped for, and it looked as good as it felt. Needless to say, I don't think I took the thing off until one day at the bus station.

I was there to catch a bus, and another young man caught my eye. It was a cold day, and he was in a sleeveless shirt. We talked a little bit, and he commented on what a sweet jacket I had, and in my humility, I'm sure I said, I know, right?

When my bus arrived, and I was departing for the warm interior to take my trip, I looked back and there he was. Six hours was what he said. He had six hours to wait in the cold until his bus came. He'd spent his last penny just to get on it, and he stood shivering.

It was like I could hear Echo echoing in my head. "Give him the coat Kelly, you know you want to do it! He needs it, and you'll feel bad if you leave him there cold."

It was a lie. I didn't "want" to give him my coat. For one thing, it contained a big bag of my Grandmother's homemade cookies, and I know, you're all thinking your grandmother makes the best, but you do not even understand. For a chubby guy to give up a coat is not that big of a deal, we have insulation, but food? That was taking it too far, but I knew that's what I had to do.

So, as the bus pulled out and I took one last look at that jacket, I sank back into the seat with a smile. She was right again. I did feel good about it. I never did replace that jacket. It was as if just owning it for a bit was enough. I'd had my dream and found something greater, love.

Reckless love for a stranger had completely replaced the "love" I thought I had for an NFL starter jacket with my team's logo on it.

In this is love, that while we were still sinners, Christ died for us. That's reckless. It wasn't a sure thing; it wasn't even a very good trade, His perfect, sinless perfection, for me.

The Bible is filled with pictures of Reckless Love, and as we start this journey, I'm going to share three of what I think are the greatest examples. They inform what we do a lot, and I share them nearly everywhere I go in one way or another. They embody the spirit of our work and show God's work in some miraculous ways.

Before I go further, I feel like I need to share one more point here. Recklessly Loving isn't about you, or just that person, even. It's not about loving just because you can, want, or feel compelled to. It isn't just about being a humanitarian. It's a direct reflection of the WHY of Reckless Love Revolution. Because He first loved us.

Just as my mom was constantly reminding me, it's not just because it feels good; it's because people need to know, Jesus loved them first.

So, while I often try to remain anonymous with my acts of Reckless Love, I also try to leave a little reminder of the why. Early on, I realized, I needed a tool that could share this message, even when I didn't feel like sticking around to take credit. So, we came up with something called a why card. This little card is the size of a business card, and it says, "WHY?" on the front, and "To find out WHY visit www.Reck-lessLoveRevolution.com" (*this site is no longer active*) on the back. I leave these, wherever God calls me to be recklessly loving. But it's not a tract, you can't just leave these in a mailbox, under a windshield wiper, or with a cashier, or a waitress. You have to first actively love someone like Jesus. You have to love them so recklessly that they are forced to ask, "why"?

It's my hope that people follow-up and investigate the card. Most, in America, have heard the story and will understand what it means. That doesn't seem to make it any less shocking, and these little cards get some amazing responses, but I'll share more on that later and how you can start using this tool too!

Now, let's dive into God's word and take a look under the hood of this Reckless Love thing at some amazing stories that impact me differently every single time I share them. In case you still don't get it yet, I'll start out with the best example of Reckless Love I think in all of Scripture, and it's not big, or flashy, it's really simple, it's something any of us can do. Give all of what you've got.

One day, Jesus was hanging with the disciples, and He took them to the temple. He liked to use worship as a teaching tool, and as they wandered through the temple courts, He stopped near where a collection box stood for tithes.

See, in the Levitical law, the tithe was used for three things. One was to support the Levites and Priests, who maintained the temple and conducted all of the required worship sacraments and sacrifices. Since these families gave up their birthright and didn't own property, or engage in business, they received one-third of the tithe as their support.

Another, lesser-known part, was reserved for celebrating feasts. God wanted His people to rejoice in Him, so He instructed them to set one-third of it aside for feasting and celebrating at times and places He instructed.

Last, but not least, was the poor, strangers that were in their land, and the widows and orphans. One-third of the tithe was to be set aside to help them survive, and that part is kind of important in this story.

As Jesus stood with His disciples, they watched as different people moved up to the box and dropped in their offerings. Some made a big show, some seemed to give grudgingly, and then there were those that really seemed to get it.

First, a man in fine robes, who had opened a full, elegant leather purse, making a show out of counting and clattering his gold coins into the box, in a prideful show of his self-righteous, religiosity, which I'm sure Judas was impressed with.

Next, came a stooped, old woman, all alone.

Jesus nudged the disciples and nodded toward her.

From her dress and demeanor, they could see that she was a widow, possibly still in mourning. Jesus watched intently, wanting them to pay close attention. And as the woman approached the box with some difficulty, she withdrew a small, cloth purse, worn with care and heavy handling. From it, she took two pennies. Without looking around to see who noticed, with a smile on her face, the woman dropped her two coins into the box.

The disciples stood, wondering what it meant. So, Jesus explained it, but first, let me set this in a more modern context to be sure you understand.

On a Sunday, we walk quietly into the back of the sanctuary of a small church, just in time to see the offering being collected. the minister sets a box where members can walk up and leave their contributions, instead of passing a plate. One by one, people step forward, some happily, others weary and fearful, until a man in an Armani suit stands up. He walks to the front and pulls out his black card.

"You do take plastic, right preacher? How much do you need, you know, to run this place for a couple of months or so? Whatever you need, just say the word."

The minister appears embarrassed and explains that he can't take the credit card. So, the man sighs, and grins, and pulls out a money clip, filled to capacity with crisp hundreds. He peels them off, one at a time, making a show out of stuffing each bill into the box, after holding it up. Finally, he's fulfilled his obligation, and as he turns to leave, for good measure, he stuffs one more bill into the minister's suit pocket.

"Get yourself something nice," he says, swaggering back down the aisle, all eyes on his Gucci loafers as he exits the building, stopping only to collect his trophy wife.

The congregation seems in awe. They whisper among themselves, and just as the minister is about to take the collection box back to its place, a woman stands up.

The congregation grows restless. No one wants to look at her, for fear they'll have to help. She's dressed in a simple black dress, and you remember, you saw her picture in the paper. Her husband has recently died, and her business was closed down due to debts he had never told her about. It's no wonder everyone avoids her gaze. They either feel guilty, or ashamed for doing little to help. She stands up, and as she moves past, toward the aisle, she says.

"Father, this is my last two dollars, and I don't know what we'll eat tonight, but I know You're a rewarder of those who seek You. You also said You love a cheerful giver and I know, that as tough as things are, there are others that need help even more than I do, so I gladly give this up. Please meet me where I am."

She completes her journey and tucks the money into the offering box; no one looks at her as she walks, smiling through tears from the sanctuary, expecting God to do amazing things with her gift.

Jesus looked at His disciples and asked, "Who gave the greater gift? Was it the wealthy merchant, who gave out of his abundance a tiny fraction of what he could have given? No, it was the widow woman."

I'm sure some smart aleck in the group must have said something, like, "Um, well, simple math shows that's not true. She only put in two pennies, that will hardly buy a loaf of bread at today's prices, but two Levites could easily live a whole month on those gold coins. Come on; you expect us to believe ..."

"You're missing the point. He gave what he will never miss from his abundance. She gave everything she had from her need. In fact, she is the greatest giver in Israel today, and her story is going to be told wherever people meet to worship from this day on."

That's reckless love.

CHAPTER 2
"Our Love Is Like Water"
-LIVE

We all know them. They have nothing to offer. Even if God gets ahold of them, they'll never amount to much in the world's eyes. They don't fit in. They have nothing to offer. They can't write fat checks, carry on great conversations, look good in designer clothes, or create anything special.

They're throw away people who don't really amount to much. When they're gone, most of them will not even be missed much. That's the assessment they're used to. These people have existed in every age. They know they don't amount to much. They tend to stick to their own kind and stay out of the way of those who matter. But, that's not how Jesus saw it at all.

In fact, with everyone who He could have spent His time with, He chose, on purpose to visit people it made no sense to love.

Jesus was only here for such a short time, and when you look at the years He actively ministered, it seems like only a few moments in time. So, He had to be very intentional about where He chose to share His gifts.

After all, He'd chosen to limit Himself to a finite, human body and constrict Himself to time in a mission to share the love of the Creator with His whole creation. So why did He choose so many seemingly unlovable people to share it with?

Get this. Here He was, trying to pull off a great revolution in the thinking of society. He was working to turn things on their heads. Introduce a new way of life, a new way of thinking. He should have gone to the intellectuals. There were plenty to be found in Rome. Or to the politically powerful, or the wealthy, to support His ministry.

But, instead, He chose the marginalized, the hurting, the crushed and the discarded. It's easy to assume that Jesus did this out of overwhelming compassion for their pain, or out of some sort of divine pity, recognizing they needed a kind word from Him, because no one else was giving it, but what if it was something more?

What if Jesus, just maybe, understood some things about human nature that we don't? I mean, He was there when we were created, after all. What if He saw a strategy for winning hearts and minds that was irresistible and He used it? What if He understood that these people, who stood the most to gain, and had the least to lose were the vehicle that would spread His message faster than any other?

I don't want to sound like Jesus was manipulative, and don't get me wrong, I think He did see their pain, their loneliness and brokenness drew Him in. I think He liked that they were real and honest with Him. I think He appreciated their lack of agenda and willingness to accept those that society had cast aside.

But I also think the choice was intentional, and I think it's something we often miss in the crush of our modern world. So, what did Jesus find so compelling in these people? Well, let's take a look at the time He went out of His way to have a cup of cold water with a half-breed whore, in a town He wasn't welcome in, to get a better idea of it.

I don't know where you grew up, but nearly everywhere in the world, there are towns, or neighborhoods where you don't belong. Whether it's because of the color of your skin, or the fact you don't know that Longhorn heads are sup-posed to be upside down, there are places you just should not be. Samaria was one of those places for a Hebrew, es-pecially one that wanted to have a decent public reputation. The history of the town was mixed up with Canaanites and Israel's rebellion against God's command to get rid of all of them, and their idol worship.

Samaria was one of the holdouts. It was a place that was filled with the kinds of things your mother warned you about, and every good Hebrew knew that to get from Judea to

Galilee you had to take the long way around, which took an extra three days.

Part of the problem was the people's heritage. They weren't just outsiders; they were half-breeds. When God had commanded that His people not intermarry with the Canaanites, not everyone listened, and Samaria was a town of mixed descent. The other issue was their worship. It was mixed with a little of this and a little of that so that Jewish tradition got intertwined with idol worship.

Not to mention, they made the completely audacious claim that God met them on their mountain, so they did not need to go to the temple, which was tough for them anyway since they weren't welcome there.

So, when Jesus set off to Galilee, everyone would have assumed He'd be a good little Jew and take the long way home.

Except they didn't know Jesus very well.

He was never very good at meeting expectations, or coloring inside of manmade lines, or following rules in the way He was told to. I love this about Jesus!

While He had the right to just tear down human authority and reshuffle the whole deck, instead, He flew in the face of convention to try and make a point, which is why He ended up in Samaria, tired and thirsty, standing beside a well.

But, here's what John records about this journey and it makes me smile every single time.

Jesus had to go through Samaria. It's a recorded fact that there was another route, traditionally taken by those who wanted to stay pure. It led all the way around the Samaritan's mountain, but Jesus just had to go through Samaria. I don't know if John is referring to his encounter or Jesus urgency about getting to Galilee. All it tells us is that one phrase - He had to go through this forbidden zone.

Samaria was a group of small towns, and Jesus knew where he was headed. He pulled off the road to rest his sandals at a little burg called Sychar. If you're like me and you grew up in small towns, you know the kind of place this is. Everyone knows everyone and everyone's business.

Sychar was situated near a Jewish holy site, called Jacob's well. If you read the Bible, you know that God changed Jacob's name to Israel, and he was considered the father of the entire Hebrew nation.

So, here's Jesus, tired and thirsty, in the hottest part of the day, with the sun straight over head near noon, sitting near the well and waiting for someone to come out of the town to draw water.

Before we go any further, let's talk a little about what would have been expected from a Jewish man, especially a prophet of God in those days. First, he should have never gone anywhere near this region; it was best avoided entirely.

Second, it was completely taboo for a man to talk to an un-accompanied woman to whom he was unrelated.

Finally, the woman Jesus is about to encounter was the kind of girl who will give you a bad reputation just getting seen with her in the hall beside your locker, if you know what I mean.

The disciples, meanwhile, had gone into Sychar to buy some food from the market and left Jesus there, beside the well. As He's sitting there, a woman came out of Sychar, carrying a watering jar.

Now, the Bible doesn't tell us anything about what this woman looked like, but, if it were today, I'm going to make some guesses. She had that look of a woman who's been around the block a few times. She probably sized Jesus up and gave him a flirty look, out of habit, not true interest. You've met people like her, they've managed to weaponize sexuality for their own defense, and they exude seduction, without even intending to.

So, Jesus says, "Hey girl." (Just picture Ryan Gosling in sandals and a beard and go with me, here.)

He says, "Hey girl, can I get a drink from your water jar? I'm parched."

She had probably heard this line before, and by now it's dawned on her that He might have read her first glance as flirting and things were getting awkward, so she answers Him.

"Are You sure You should be talking to me? You know I'm a half-breed, right? Aren't You a Jew? You really don't want any part of the trouble that comes with knowing me."

I'm paraphrasing here, but you get the picture. In context, this isn't as simple as it seems. The act of drawing water requires some labor. She's got to drop a heavy clay jar into the well on a rope, let it fill and then drag it back out. It's as if Jesus has wandered into a modern-day bar, on the wrong side of town and asked the first woman to walk up to buy Him a drink.

"You're a Jew. Aren't You a long way from home? How can You ask a Samaritan woman for a drink? Don't You care at all what people think of You?"

Now, if this woman didn't already think He was there for "other purposes," what Jesus said next would have almost sealed the deal. If this were any other man in the history of the world, this would come out as the cheesiest pickup line of all time. "You don't know who I am, huh? If you understood God's gift, and who I am, you would be asking me for a drink. I would give you living water."

Now obviously, what Jesus meant here must have been something completely different than how that comes across in the modern context, but still, confusing.

I would love to someday meet this woman and just ask her, what did you think was going on? We get a bit of a clue in her next reply because she continues to banter a bit. I can just see a tired smile come across her face, that doesn't quite reach her eyes and hear a little sarcastic half laugh, she's heard it all before.

"Oh, really? How are You going to do that? I don't see a water jar there, hotshot. This well is pretty deep, so where are You going to get this "living water" You're so sure about? You know our ancestor Jacob built this place and drank from it, and watered his livestock here. Are you trying to say You're better than him?"

The mention of Jacob here is interesting. She's drawing him out. Jacob was a shared piece of history between the two of them. They were both his descendants and it kind of feels like she's trying to change the conversation while looking over her shoulder, either hoping for help to come along or hoping no one sees her talking to this crazy person.

Jesus doubles down.

"Look, if I were to draw water from this well and give you a drink, you'd just want more an hour from now. But, with the water I'm offering, you'd never be thirsty again. In fact, it would bubble up inside of you to provide you a never-ending supply."

This is where the conversation turns the corner and Jesus is about to set up the spike and show this woman a whole new kind of love than what she might be thinking right about now. I could just see the sarcastic grin slip, and her tired eyes show a glimmer of hope. He's not hitting on her, that much is sure, but is He crazy, or for real? She looks into His eyes, and her guard drops, instantly. She can see that He's serious.

"Um, wow. I don't normally do things like this with strange Jewish men, but give me this water you're talking about. I'm so tired of drawing water from this well. Seriously, how can I get some?"

"I tell you what, go get your husband and come back," Jesus says.

It almost feels like He's giving the nod to the way things are supposed to be done here. The men can talk business.

The woman's half grin comes back up, her armor was slipping, but she retreats just a little, "I don't have a husband." Jesus smiles, warmly, and I don't think He says this in an accusing tone at all, "I know. But, you have had five husbands, and the man you live with now is not your husband. You're finally letting down your guard enough to tell me the truth."

I picture her, water jar on the edge of the well, about to draw some out, when she freezes and turns white. Her eyes narrow. She's trying to sort out who this guy is and how He knows so much about her. If she was a city girl, she might just assume she'd met Him before, but in this tiny town, Jesus would stand out. He didn't dress like them, look like them, or even talk like them. She knew He'd never been there.

Now, remember, this was before Facebook, so it's doubtful He was one of those creeper "friends" who you forget about until they give a random reply to a post that has nothing to do with the reason for posting it. That only left one option. As she stood there, completely undone by His gaze, a realization that He had not been talking about physical water started to sink in.

Trembling, she comes toward Him a little, "Well, You're no ordinary man. You obviously have a prophetic gift, but You need to know something. My family has been worshipping right here on this mountain for generations. But, Your people claim we have to leave here and go to the temple to find God."

She sticks it out there like a test. She's pretty sure this conversation is about to go south, and she wants to get it over with.

He hadn't called her a whore. He hadn't refused to engage her in conversation. It was obvious there was something powerful in Him, but why was He here? It couldn't be just for her. She didn't deserve His attention. I think she knew the presence of God, from her own worship. She recognized it in Jesus but was confused why He would come to her, a forbidden woman, in a forbidden place, and now she's expecting Him to judge her relationship with God, but He doesn't.

Watch this.

I picture Jesus smiling gently here. She understands something is happening and He doesn't want to scare her away from what He's about to do for her.

"Soon, you won't have to be here, or in Jerusalem to worship our Father. I see that you worship something you don't quite understand. We Jews know God, and salvation comes through us, but there's a time coming when true worshippers will be able to worship God in their spirits, and in truth, no matter where they are. This is what God wants, honest, true hearts that worship Him in Spirit and truth. Our Father is pure Spirit, and anyone who wants to worship Him must do it in Spirit and truth."

It was like Jesus had just revealed everything she'd always suspected about God in one brief instant. I can almost see the woman's eyes filling with tears of gratitude for His kindness. At this point, she knows who Jesus is, but she has to ask.

"I know that Messiah is coming and He will explain everything to us when He arrives."

Jesus comes to the woman and smiles, "You're right. I'm the Messiah, and I just did."

The disciples have some of the most epic timing in history. Right here, in the middle of this beautiful moment, they show up with food. Can you imagine it? They probably told Him they shouldn't go through Samaria, they may have warned Him about what people would think, and now, not only did He go there, but He's at the public well, talking to an unaccompanied Samaritan whore. Talk about your Jewish hat trick of public humiliation.

They didn't know what to say, and in an uncharacteristically clear moment, they made a really wise choice.

They said nothing.

This was pretty rare for the disciples. They were kind of famous for saying the wrong thing, like that time they tried to keep the kids from coming to Jesus? Somehow, they were either too embarrassed or sensed that something good was about to happen.

The woman, though, couldn't stop talking. She left the well and ran to town.

Remember at the beginning of the chapter, I told you that Jesus had an agenda in picking her? Well, this is where we get to see a glimpse of it. Instead of hiding what happened, or looking for just the right person to tell, this woman, rid of her shame for the first time in who knows how long, goes along the city street, telling people.

"Hey, this man out by the well, He knows everything I've ever done! I think He's the Messiah!"

Had it been anyone else, I wonder, would if it have had the same impact? If what He'd been able to see in this woman had been praise worthy and honorable, would people have reacted as they did?

You'd expect, given the woman's history, that anyone who could see what she'd done would shame her. But, here she was, laughing and grinning about it. Somehow, what she was saying made sense. If someone could "read her mail" and make her feel good about it, maybe there was something to this.

So, they all went to the well.

Meanwhile, the disciples return to their normal selves and start telling Jesus what to do. "Hey, Teach, You need to have a sandwich or something."

"I'm good, I've got food that you don't know about." He smiled.

Right here, this is what I'm talking about.

Just moments before, they were sensitive enough to keep their comments to themselves, but here they go.

"Where did He get food?"

"I don't know, maybe that woman brought Him something?"

"Surely not, you don't think..."

I really think that when they wrote this stuff down, years later, they left these moments in so that we could feel good about ourselves. They were human. It kind of makes you feel like maybe you really could serve God. After all, guys like Peter, James and John did it.

Jesus has committed an act of Reckless Love, risking His reputation to come out of His way to love a woman that didn't make sense to love and here these guys are arguing over where he'd gotten a snack.

I love this next bit, Jesus waxes poetic, to further confuse them.
"My food is to do what God sent Me to do."

Imagine the blank stares. They just aren't getting it, so Jesus throws a farming metaphor into the mix.

I think He must have sighed when He said this, "Don't you have a saying, it's four more months until harvest? Look around! The fields are ready to be plucked! Right now, harvesters can reap an eternal crop, so that those who spread the seed and those who pick the fruit can rejoice together! This is what's meant by the saying, one plants, another harvests. I sent you out to harvest what you didn't plant. Others have already prepared the crops for you and done the hard work. You're earning the rewards of their labor."

So, while the disciples are sorting out what the heck Jesus is talking about, the Samaritans come out of the city and gather around the well. They invite Jesus to stay, so he does. He spends two more days teaching in Sychar, and a lot of the town believe in Him. Seeking out this one woman, that it seemingly made no sense to love, leads an entire town to faith.

But that's not all.

Jesus continues on His way to Galilee, and get this, Remember how we said the traditional route a Jew should take around Samaria would take three days? His little detour through Samaria, puts Him right on schedule! Even though He stayed to teach for two more days, He ends up right where He would have been, if He was a good little Jew and followed protocol to protect His reputation.

It's funny how things work out when we follow God's call to Reckless Love.

He uses the simple things of this world to confuse the wise, and I'm convinced that loving those it makes no sense to love, is one of those things. Never prejudge a recipient of your acts of Reckless Love. Let God lead, and you follow.

CHAPTER 3
"Your Love Has Rescued Me"
- Verses

There's something I think people miss about Jesus when they're figuring out who He was and what He was about. They make the mistake of framing Him in religious terms. But, see, that's a problem, because Jesus Himself said very little about "religion" or systems of belief. He told stories, most of them allegories, or parables, and almost none of them were even overtly spiritual, let alone religious.

He simplified what the Pharisees wanted to complicate and that ticked them off to no end. In the process of turning the existing structure on its head, He put a lot of emphasis on the value of the individual, something that didn't make a lot of sense in the ancient world. Some of the stories He told were specifically designed to point this out. He wanted to show that in the kingdom He was establishing, each member would be just as important as the next. So He went out of His way to drive this point home.

He liked to use agricultural metaphors that the people of Galilee could understand and one of His favorites was sheep and shepherds. He painted a picture of Himself as being a Good Shepherd, a demeaning, but a necessary profession in that time. He said that a good shepherd didn't just show concern for the flock, but for each sheep.

"It's like this," He said (I'm paraphrasing again). "If a good shepherd drives his flock home after a day of grazing and as he goes to pen them up, he counts 99 when there had been a hundred, he's not satisfied with that."

In business, a one percent loss in inventory is often completely overlooked in the pursuit of profit. As long as the bottom line adds up, we often don't bother with a single stray, but not Jesus.

"In fact," He said, "the good shepherd won't stay with the 99 who are safe at home. He won't consider the long day he's already had, or how he'd like to just go home to his supper, his wife, and his warm bed. He'll grab a torch and his staff and head off into the darkness to find it."

If you've ever spent any time in the wilderness, you know that wandering around in the dark, is just about the best way to end up food for something. Jesus insisted it wouldn't matter to Him when it came to His sheep. He would wander the hillsides until He found that lost lamb, then carry it home, as tired as He was, over His own shoulders.

Now, remember, it's not like a shepherd could just sleep in the next morning. That's not how it works. When you're tending herds, they dictate the schedule, so, sleep, or no sleep, the good shepherd would be back out the next day, doing it all over again.

As I've thought about Reckless Love and the vision I want to share with people wherever I go, I've made it a point to communicate that we should never, under any circumstances, underestimate the value of even one, solitary person. Jesus didn't, and I won't either.

It wasn't just in His stories that Jesus dealt with this topic, though, He modeled it in everyday life as well.

Maybe one of the most extreme examples was the story of the Gadarene Demoniac. It just sounds like an epic tale, doesn't it? I mean, can't you just hear adventurers around a fire asking their "bard" to sing the Ballad of the Gadarene Demoniac? It's an epic idea for a band name too. Anyway, here's what happened.

In the height of His ministry, basically, anywhere that Jesus sat down for five minutes, people showed up and asked Him to teach them things. He could be in a small town, or a city, or out on the side of a mountain. It didn't matter. Somehow, without cell phones, or landlines, or the internet, hashtags, or Snapchat, people found out.

It was like the ancient equivalent of a nineties rave. All the cool kids knew where the action was, and Jesus was in the center of it.

So, He was on the hillside with His disciples when a crowd gathers. Over 5000 people. In fact, unless you count Moses with the children of Israel in the desert, this might have been the first ever megachurch. So, after preaching to this huge congregation, Jesus is wiped out.

He decides they need a little R&R, so, like any red-blooded male, He heads to the lake to find a boat and get away from it all.

Now, the Bible doesn't say this, but I get the feeling He knew where He was going, because this demoniac dude is there, waiting to greet Him, but I'm getting ahead of myself.

Night falls as they're sailing out across this lake and a storm comes up. Remember, this boat full of dudes grew up in a water-born culture. They lived on the shores of this great lake, and several of them were even professional fishermen.

I don't know if you've ever watched "Greatest Catch" or not, but, those fellas are bad to the bone. They don't scare easy, so I'm guessing the Bible kind of downplays this next part. It mentions waves and says they were afraid of the boat capsizing, and that's about it. But, you can imagine, they've hauled in the sail, turned the boat into the wind, they're steering into the waves, and whatever ancient Mediterranean sailors did to survive this stuff, they've tried it. I can't picture them giving up easy; it was probably hours of fighting the rain and waves before they just decided they were lost.

Let's face it guys. If they were going to ask Jesus for help, it was desperate. Think about it. Think of the hard men you know in your life. The guys who earn their living with their sweat and skin. They don't back down, and they don't give up, and they certainly never, ever, ask for help. So, things were desperate by this point, but where's Jesus?
Can you picture it?

Here's James and John at the wheel of the boat, wiping spray from their eyes and trying to see as best they can into the dark, hoping for a star or something to at least tell them which way to point. They were called the sons of thunder, so I imagine the language that night was "colorful" to say the least when here comes little tax collector Peter.

Picture it. Two tough sailors, being approached by an accountant.

"Guys, maybe we need to get Jesus?"

By this point, they're exhausted, and they agree. So, Phillip goes looking for Him. Finally, they find Him, curled up with a net for a pillow, His cloak pulled up over His head, snoring peacefully at the very front of the boat, the part that is taking the bulk of the pounding. So, they wake Him up.

"Uh, Jesus, we've got a little problem here. James and John are worried this boat is going under, what should we do?"

I picture Jesus opening one eye, having His dreams of being back home in heaven interrupted. He doesn't look real happy. So, He stands up, shakes the rain from His cloak. His shoulders go up and down in a massive sigh as He looks at them, then up to the sky with a, "Really, Father, are these the right guys?" kind of look.

"Peace! Be still!" He says, calmly.

And instantly, the rain stops. The winds subside, and the sea goes still all around them. Where there had been nothing but fog, and clouds and mist, was a clear night, the moon overhead and the stars reflecting off the still surface of the lake, with the sun just rising over the horizon.

Then, Jesus, I'm guessing, goes back to sleep.

So, they start talking about it, "Who is this guy? I've never seen anything like that before."

But what had just happened could in no way prepare them for the dude Jesus was going to see. If you have never come face to face with a person under the direct influence of an evil spirit, trust me, no storm compares to what was about to go down.

The rest of the voyage is calm and peaceful, and they pull up onto a beach, just outside a graveyard. The area they were in was inhabited by a group of people known as the

Gesarenes, and it was called Decapolis. Literally translated to English, it means, "Ten cities."

Jesus no sooner puts a foot on the sand than this crazy eyed, wild haired, homeless guy marches up to Him, and even the disciples, not always the sharpest knives in the drawer, could obviously see something was up with this dude. He was shaggy and dirty from living out in the tombs, and his body was scratched and bloody and bruised, from bashing himself with rocks on these wild binges he would go on, running off into the wilderness.

It's likely he was dragging ropes or chains behind him as he approached since the Bible says they were constantly trying to tie this guy down so he wouldn't hurt himself or anyone else. But even their strongest chains wouldn't hold him.

This makes you think; he was probably jacked. But, my guess, he was one of those crazy strong skinny little dudes, and the demons inside him, just made him that much stronger.

However it had started, we don't know, but this poor guy hadn't been in his right mind in a while. We're told that they got sick of him in the city. They just couldn't control him. So, out of fear of the spirits that lived inside him, they moved him out where he couldn't hurt anybody, into the cemetery. That's where he'd been chained and broken free from so many times that they had finally given up.

Now Jesus already knows the score here, and He immediately commands the spirits to let go of this man and come out, but they decide to negotiate. First thing the dude does is take a look at Jesus and instantly recognize Him,

"Jesus? What are You doing here? Have You come to torture us?"

The sharpest of the disciples are catching on. This isn't the first demon-possessed man they've seen, and him referring to himself as "us" was a big clue. So they explain it to the slower ones, like Peter and Thomas, who always seemed the last to catch on.

"What is your name?" Jesus asks.

And I think He was reaching out to the man, hidden inside this shell of a body, letting him know, "I see you in there."

But, instead, the spirits answer.

"Well, there's a bunch of us in here, and we've decided to call ourselves 'Legion,'" the man says.

I find this next part kind of ironic. Here the demons' have just used this mega-tough sounding moniker to refer to themselves in the plural, putting on a show of strength, but Jesus isn't fazed. They recognize this pretty quick and throw this poor man down onto his knees in front of Jesus and start begging for their existence.

"Please! If you're going to cast us out, don't banish us! Look, we know you're a Jew, and don't care much for pigs, so, how about this? We'll leave this guy. He can have his body back, you win! Only, send us into the pigs, that way we don't have to leave. Deal?"

I think Jesus smirks, and maybe rolls His eyes a little, "Fine, get out!"

I've always wondered why Jesus would answer the request of the demons in this story. I've never been able to find an answer for this though I've searched many commentaries and reference materials. But what I've come to take from this is, if Jesus is willing to answer the request of demons, how much more willing is He to answer the request of those He loves and gave His life for! Just think about that for a minute.

And that was all it took. Just a few words from Jesus and the demons left. But, things were just starting to get interesting here in Decapolis. The instant the demons hit the pigs, the pigs freaked out. Remember, they were on the shore of the Sea of Galilee, and the pigs wanted nothing to do with this. They did what animals do when they find themselves under attack from something they can't fight back against - they ran. The Bible tells us they ran to the nearest cliff and took a flying leap into the sea and drown.

By this time, a crowd had started to gather, and they had seen what was going on. So, they started spreading the word, and more people began to arrive out here in the grave yard.

And I'm guessing the disciples were already sizing them up, guessing what sermon Jesus was going to preach. Wondering if He'd pull the loaves and fishes stunt again, and Judas was busily calculating what kind of offering they might expect. But, that's not what was going down today.

Jesus had literally crossed the lake in the middle of the night, risking all their lives, to speak into one man's life. This demon possessed man, who was now freed, would be the only one to welcome them there that day.

In fact, the people who showed up took one look at their former friend, who now seemed sane, and they were scared spitless. If you think about it, this is a pretty logical reaction. It stands to reason if they had tried everything to heal this guy, and nothing had worked, that whatever power Jesus had used, it was something to be respected and feared.

I'm sure the pig farmer didn't help, "We need to get rid of him! He's already ruined my business, and who knows whose herd he'll kill next?"

Very quickly, a consensus was formed, the people of Decapolis wanted nothing to do with Jesus and His band of followers. In fact, not only were they not going to ask Him to preach, they told Him to leave. To me, this is kind of cool, because of what Jesus does. He leaves.

I know, some of you are saying, wait a minute Kelly K, why would He do that? Didn't they need to hear what He said? Well, I think we could all learn a lesson here about respecting the rights of our fellow man.

Here's Jesus, Creator of the universe, just freed them from a really big headache, and destroyed a non-kosher food source, being shown the door. But, He doesn't react as you might expect. He just smiles and walks back to the boat.

See, Jesus understood something that many times we don't seem to get when it comes to sharing the gospel.

It's a free gift.

And anyone is free to accept, or reject it. He honored that here. But, as usual, He also had another little strategy brewing on the side. While the people of Decapolis thought if they could rid themselves of Jesus, they wouldn't have to deal with whatever He was selling. They had discounted the value of the one man Jesus had come to see.

So, the disciples are getting the boat ready, and the crowd is gathering on the shore, chanting slogans and throwing rocks, " What do we want?" "Jesus gone!" "When do want it?" "Right now!" but Legion, he's still following them.

"Hey, guys, hold up. Look, Jesus, about what happened back there, thank you so much! I owe You my life, so, I'm coming with You. I can't stay here."

Jesus stops there on the shore and gives this guy a mission. There was a reason He had come all the way across the lake on a stormy night to see this guy, and we're going to see him again in a bit.

Jesus takes a look at him, "Listen, friend, I know you want to help Me. So, here's what I need you to do. I need you to go back. Because what just happened to you is what they need to hear. Look at them. They are not in the mood to listen to Me right now, but they won't be able to argue with what you've got to share. So, can you do that for Me? Since I can't preach here, will you be My voice and tell everyone here what happened to you?"

I can just see this poor guy, recently returned to his senses, but with all the horrible memories of what they'd done to him there in their own self-defense. He must have been bummed at first, looking from the angry, scared crowd, back to the ship.

But something inside him lit a fire. I can imagine him nod-ding, a determined look coming across his face, "Yeah, yeah, I think I can do that. It's the least I can do for what You did for me...thank You!"

And as the tiny ship pulled out into the sea, the angry crowd dropped their rocks. One by one, they turned for home, while Legion stood there on the shore, waving until their sails disappeared across the horizon.

See, Jesus knew that out of all the people in the Ten Cities, He only needed one, and we'll talk more about what happens there a little later in this book.

God is constantly challenging me with this thought, don't discount the one. Don't stay with the 99, go after the one. The value of just one soul can outweigh the dangers of the storm at sea, and the angry opinions of cities filled with fearful, angry people and turn the situation around. Even if all that happened was setting this one man free, imagine the impact. He could rejoin his family and live a normal life. Even if he never says a word, the story is going to travel.

In God's kingdom, every "one" is important. There is no one more important than another.

Jesus said that in eternity, there is more celebrating over one soul that discovers the truth, than over all of those who are already in the kingdom. That's a pretty powerful statement. One soul can equal the entire host of heaven.

The Good Shepherd knew that when he left behind the 5000, braved the sea to free a man and was met with hostility and fear. It was okay. He'd found the one lamb he'd set out to rescue, and for that one, things would never be the same.

CHAPTER 4
"You Will Be Caught Off-Guard, Floored By Love"
- Maria Mena

The third and final big idea behind Reckless Love Revolution is all about our agendas. As human beings, and particularly as Americans, we are taught to make our lives revolve around us.

Now, I know, this may seem to be contrary to the idea of the value of one, but it's got to be said. While the gospel is about each of us, individually, the kingdom can never be about our own selfish agenda.

There have been so many times in my life that God has had to remind me not to be frustrated by interruptions in His service.

It's not that He doesn't care about what I want. The Bible is filled with examples of how much He wants to give me what I want. It's not that my time isn't important and others shouldn't respect the priorities I've set. It's an idea that's kind of wrapped up in the first two.

When God speaks to send me on a mission, it's often an interruption of my plans. I've got some other end in mind, and He needs me to take a little detour. It's easy for me to forget whose project this is in the first place, and assert my "rights" where they don't belong.

I've been bought with a price, and my life is not my own any longer. It's tough to remember that.

The best example of this I find in Scripture comes at the beginning of the church. Things have just gotten off the ground after the resurrection and ascension. The Holy Spirit has fallen on the disciples, and things have gotten pretty tough Jerusalem and the surrounding territory. In fact, one disciple, Stephen, has been publicly stoned to death for preaching about Jesus and it's getting dangerous for believers to be seen together.

Men like Saul of Tarsus (if you don't know who that is, his name was later changed to Paul, and he wrote a lot of the New Testament) were actively seeking to kill believers. So the church in Jerusalem decided the best thing to do was to spread out. The believers scattered out from Jerusalem and began to share what they had learned about Jesus.

Phillip was one of these men.

Phillip chose an interesting mission field. He went back to a place we've already talked about quite a bit, Samaria. After his friend Stephen was stoned, Phillip realized he couldn't stay in Jerusalem, so he packed up and headed somewhere he figured the Pharisees wouldn't follow him. His message was well received in Samaria, and he spent some time casting out evil spirits, which, it turns out (as we saw in the last chapter), is a great way to draw a crowd.

But, this time, the people were appreciative. In fact, it seemed that the miracles God performed through Phillip were just the thing they needed to see to make him credible and they started listening to him carefully. So many people were believing and being baptized that word got back to Peter and John in Jerusalem, and they were sent by the church there to join Phillip.

Phillip's ministry was really taking off and with the addition of John and Peter, came the anointing of the Holy Spirit.

As they met with new believers in Samaria, they would lay hands on them and ask the Holy Ghost to fill them, and He did. In fact, it drew the attention of an interesting character. In the same city where Phillip was preaching, there was a man known as a mystic, a magician by the name of Simon, that the people sought out as a prophet. They believed he could hear from and speak for God. Simon had heard Phillip preach, and he'd been baptized as a believer in Jesus. But he still had an eye out for ways to make money with his "gift," and this Holy Spirit gig seemed like just the thing. So, while other believers were accepting it with an open heart, and using it to heal the sick and do other good things, Simon wanted to cash in. He came to John and Peter with a proposition.

"Look, fellas. I saw what you were doing there, and that's pretty cool. I'm a practitioner of the spiritual arts myself, and I could share that with a lot of people. So, I thought you could probably use some 'funding for your ministry' (wink, wink); am I right, or am I right? So, what do you say, guys? Can I get in on this?"

If you've spent much time studying the New Testament, you know Peter was not one to be overly diplomatic in his responses, and this guy was really getting on his nerves.

"You know what? To hell with you and your money. If you think you can buy the gift of God, you're not fit to be a part of this. You need a come-to-Jesus moment, apparently. In fact, I'd suggest you pray, right now, that God forgives you before you end up like Annanias and Sapphira!"

(I'm taking some license here, but it was Peter, so, if he didn't say it, he thought it.) I can just see John calming him down.

Simon must have been a little freaked out by Peter's response.

His reply hints at the fact that he was pretty scared, "Please, pray for me so that nothing you've said happens to me."

We don't hear any more from Simon after that, but Phillip continues to preach a bang-up revival throughout Samaria and Peter and John return to Jerusalem, stopping off in a few cities to preach as well. And right in the middle of this awesome thing that Phillip was doing, a really good, "God" thing, God changes his plans.

He sends an angel to talk to Phillip.

"Go to the desert and hang out for a bit."

This is where a lot of us start to bargain with God. Most of the time it's not as clear as an angelic visitation, so we also question if it's really Him.

"Well, God, I need confirmation from at least two sources if this is really You."

"But, You sent me here to do this, they really like me and..."

We know when it's Him. We like to pretend like it's hard to figure out. But, His sheep hear His voice, and when a thought that you didn't think pops into your head to do something good, where else is it coming from? That's not to say we can't also get distracted, but you'll know the difference. When it's a distraction, it's what you want to do, and you're trying to convince yourself the other direction. An interruption almost always costs us something.

In Phil's case, it was his ministry in Samaria, at least for the moment.

For those who answer a call to full-time gospel ministry, it's easy to think we know the formula. We tend to believe that the Spirit is flowing more heavily when things seem to be going our way, but take a look at Scripture, and you'll find out quickly, that's not so. Elijah on Mount Carmel was right in the flow, but life sucked! Things were going great for Phillip, but God had other plans, and it pays to pay attention when He is the one doing the interrupting.

If you think about it, bargaining with God at a moment like this is kind of telling your boss, who set you on the task you're on, that they're wrong for moving you to something else. It's His gig, never forget that. Some of the best things that happen in Scripture were interruptions.

Think about it. Abraham wasn't considering a move. Gideon hadn't even considered a military career. Mary wasn't planning to have a child. God showed up, interrupted the normal course of things and that's when the good stuff started to happen.

So, the angel drops in on Phil while he's preaching this revival in Samaria and hands him some map coordinates. Now, this is important. See, Phil's timing here is crucial because of what God is about to do. It's easy to think, "Well, this is a God thing, it will keep until next week." Not always. Had Phillip not been willing to pack up his tent and cancel his future engagements to hit the road, he would have missed it. Check this out.

"Go south to the road that runs through the desert between Jerusalem and Gaza."

That's it. That's all he got. Sometimes God operates on a "need to know" basis and our need to know the details is very low. He's spot checking us for obedience. Besides, if He had told Phillip, "Look, I know this is going great, and you're reaching thousands, but if you think it's worth your time, I've got this guy headed down into Africa and need someone to take a meeting with him in the desert." Phillip might have made a judgment call and stayed where he was.

So, Phillip, having seen so many miraculous things in such a short time, sets out on faith at the moment he receives the message.

This is so crucial. He doesn't stop to think about what's being interrupted, he goes. It just so happens that someone was headed south along that road, that would change a lot for a whole lot of people and if Phillip had paused to eat a meal, or say goodbye, or… You get where I'm going with this. Back then, the fastest way to travel was by horse, unless you had a chariot. You've seen them in the movies. If not, get "Ben Hur." You'll thank me. A chariot is the equivalent of a Bugatti Chiron, which, if you don't know, comes in at over 1500 horses under the hood, and might just be the first pro- duction model to ever top out over 270 MPH.

Mind, you, we're later told that the Eunuch "Gives an order for the chariot to stop," so, this is not Ben Hur's stripped down racing model, more of the Cadillac variety.

Meanwhile, Phillip, on foot, is the equivalent of a Smart Car. But, the angel's timing was perfect, and good ole Phil ends up on that south road, just as the chariot is trekking south for Ethiopia.

See, the man in question, was a devout follower of the God of Israel, and a Eunuch in service of Candice, the queen of one of the wealthiest nations on earth at the time, Ethiopia. As he's riding along in his luxury horsemobile, he's reading. That doesn't seem like a big deal in our world, but remember, whatever he's reading it had to be hand copied, and those manuscripts were very rare. In this case, he's reading a piece from Isaiah. Since the poetry here is cool, I won't attempt to improve it for the modern audience. I think you'll catch on.

"He was led like a sheep to the slaughter,
and as a lamb before its shearer is silent,
so he did not open his mouth.
In his humiliation, he was deprived of justice.
Who can speak of his descendants?
For his life was taken from the earth." (Acts 8:32)

From our perspective, we know that the prophet is seeing into the future here, and commenting on the recent (for

Phillip) crucifixion of Jesus, but this Eunuch has no clue. He's a Jew and hasn't heard the good news that Messiah has come, but that's where Phil comes in.

So, in this amazing feat of divine timing, God puts Phillip, one of the few people on earth at the time, who can make the connection between Isaiah's words and Jesus, right next to this guy on the road in the middle of the desert. Phillip has followed his instructions thus far precisely. He's in the right place at the right time, and he's about to get more.

"Go run up beside that chariot and stay close," he hears the Spirit say. So he does.

As he approaches, he hears this man, presumably reading in Hebrew, reading from Isaiah, and you can imagine how he felt. If you've never felt God tell you to go somewhere, or talk to someone and then had it turn out to be a "divine coincidence," you might not get the full impact. But this is one of those full-on spooky moments when the hair on your body stands on end, and you have a moment of clarity. The God of the universe is real, He's speaking, and He's speaking directly to you, revealing things you couldn't have known. Cool stuff.

Phillip pretty much knows how to take it from here. "Hey, dude, did you understand what you just read?"

The Eunuch looks up. I picture him taking off his glasses (although they hadn't been invented yet) and a slightly sarcastic smile comes across his face. Of course, in my version, the Eunuch is played by Paterson Joseph, who has the best, one-sided, sarcastic grin of all time.

"No, I must admit, it is a bit puzzling. Why? Do you understand it?"

"I know a little," Phillip says, stopping to catch his breath as the chariot screeches to a stop.

"Tell me, is Isaiah referring to himself, or someone else?"

"Move over, there's no way I can tell you all of this and keep up with your horses at the same time," Phil says, climbing aboard and helping himself to a water skin.

The same sarcastic smile comes back, but welcoming, "Help yourself."

And with a flick of the reins, the Eunuch starts the chariot up again while Phillip situates himself with the scroll and starts into his explanation.

He takes the story from Isaiah, explains the connection to Jesus, then tells the Eunuch about everything that's happened since. Not just anyone could do it. Remember, there were only 144 in the room on Pentecost when the Spirit fell, and Phillip was around for the whole deal -- from the start of Jesus ministry, until His resurrection. He's one of only a few dozen people on earth who can do this, and this Eunuch guy is going to end up being just as important.

So, our Eunuch friend eats it up. He nods along, asks questions, starts to make his own connections between Jesus and the prophets and then he starts to get excited. He believes. I think if an inkpot and quill were available, he was making notes in the margins as the horses pulled the chariot on toward Ethiopia and home, where this man was about to change the world.

As Phillip was sharing, something about baptism struck a chord with this man, and as they approached a body of water, he pulled the chariot to a stop and hopped down.

"Any reason we can't just do this right here and now?" he asked Phillip.

"Let's do this!" Phillip responded and down into the water they went.

We're not given a liturgy here of what was said, maybe nothing. Submersion in water was the Jewish custom, so Phil dunks this Eunuch, and as he comes up out of the water, Phillip disappears.

No, I'm actually not kidding this time, that's what it says. "The Spirit took Phillip."

This part gives me goose bumps a little, because, Jesus, before he leaves tells his disciples, "Greater things than these you will do."

Now, I'm not saying I've ever been teleported by the Spirit from location to location, but what I am saying is, how completely awesome is that?

Dude standing here in the water, "Where'd he go?" to his driver, "Hey, Jeeves, did you see that little Jewish guy, just dunked me in the water, then split? I'm not imagining things again, am I? I know this desert gets to me, but what just happened?"

Meanwhile, Phil carries on as if this happens every day. We are told that he "appears" at a town called Azotus and continues his revival tour all the way to Caesarea. Dude doesn't even miss a beat. I'm sure he was bummed out about that long ride back north. He's been riding in the chariot all afternoon, so now he's got even further to hoof it back, and hitchhiking hasn't been invented yet. But God's like, "Don't even sweat it." Picks our boy Phillip up and plunks him down right where he left off, preaching through the small towns.

So, what about our African friend? He gets back into his chariot with his newfound faith in Christ and goes home. We don't hear any more about him, but I'll give you a little pre-view. We'll talk more about this later, but today there are over 40 million Ethiopian Christians. I'm not saying that was all due to this one dude, but...

Just on its face, this is one of the most bizarre stories in Scripture. It is a true inspiration to me on the topic of being ready for the interruption.

Here you have two completely unrelated dudes from com-pletely separate cultures, one with the power to speak to na-tions, but some deep, unanswered questions, and another one who has those answers as a member of a growing "in-siders" club. What are the odds they would ever meet in their lifetimes?

In today's world, sure, in an airport sky lounge somewhere, these two dudes share a bistro table because it's crowded. But in Roman times, in Galilee? Think about it. The most a man could travel in a day was about thirty miles. So, while this Ethiopian dude was a jet-setter, it's unlikely Phil had seen anything beyond a few miles from his home before Je-sus. Now, they both end up in the same place at the same time at the beckoning of an angel.

The old adage, "The Lord works in mysterious ways," doesn't even begin to cover it. When Jesus just picks this guy up on his way to Galilee one day, "Hey Phil, follow me." I wonder if this incident was on His mind?

Most of the disciples reached Jesus through a friend or a brother, but Philip, James, and John were called directly. I have to believe that Jesus, playing six moves ahead, already saw this going down from the very beginning. And on some level, Phillip too saw what was going to happen with this powerful Ethiopian.

It's all a part of the intricate web of "interruptions" God weaves to work out his plans around our messy, inconsistent and sometimes downright stubborn natures.

Phillip's act of Reckless Love in response to an angelic visit, which could have just been (in the word's of the inimitable Ebenezer Scrooge), "A bit of undigested beef," turns out to be one of the coolest incidents in all of recorded Scripture. He, in turn, gets to experience "spiritual transportation" to another location. You just never know what will happen when you stay open to interruption and keep your ears and eyes open for God's messengers.

CHAPTER 5
"How Can I Love When I'm Afraid To Fall"
- Christina Perri

I hope by this point you've got a pretty good idea of what Reckless Love looks like. The Widow, with her coins; the Woman at Jacob's well; Legion chained in the catacombs of Decapolis; and Phillip on the road to Africa are some great Biblical examples.

In a tapestry as rich as Reckless Love, there are obviously more than three threads, but the human imagination works best with a little framework, which is why we narrowed it down to three simple principles when defining an act of Reckless Love.

First, we have to love those it makes no sense to love. It's not always aimed at the people you would expect. God sees so much more than we do. He knows who to pick. He knows who needs His love the most, and who will do the most with it. Like the woman at the well, we are often faced with people it makes no sense to love. Whether they come from a different social class, another culture, or even practice a different religion, we're faced with these tests. It's up to us to understand that Reckless Love doesn't even come from us. It's not ours to divvy up or dish out. We don't get to decide who deserves it and who doesn't.

We rarely get it right anyway. I remember a night in Tulsa when I was faced with this test, and I tried to fail it. I honestly did.

We've all been faced with the scammers at the gas station. They either have a gas can, or a car that's just out of sight somewhere and five bucks for gas will change their lives. They're often young and healthy, excellent candidates for a "Get a job" speech if you know what I mean. But, not always. The one thing they all seem to have in common is something else to spend your money on once they get it. I've seen them buy beer, cigarettes, candy, but rarely gasoline, and then sometimes they just disappear into the night.

On this evening, I was at the QuikTrip pump filling up when a black woman approached me. I know it shouldn't matter what color a person's skin is, but I don't think there's a human being on the planet that doesn't see it just a little differently when someone unlike them asks for help.

She was sitting in her car, and the moment I took the handle off the pump her door opened and I could feel her pitch coming from a mile away, but I saw her coming. I wasn't getting scammed on this night. I was too smart for that.

Besides, I was late to preach, and I knew that whatever this woman was going to get up to with my hard earned dollars was not going to honor God. She came at me with both barrels, tears in her eyes, asking for gas money.

But I was resolute. I looked her in the eye and said, "No."

Then me and my pride walked in to buy a quick snack so I could get to that service before the congregation started questioning why they asked me to come in the first place. I couldn't be bothered with scammers. I was on a mission from... My thoughts were interrupted.

"Are you sure she's a scammer?"
It made no sense for me to love this woman. I had a family to feed, and could list off a dozen people I knew could use help if I needed to give. Now God was giving me the third degree.

I argued back, "Yeah, God, I'm pretty sure, I've seen this before."

"Fill her car up, anyway."

"What?" I wasn't even prepared to part with a Lincoln for this game she was running, let alone a full tank. But He wasn't letting go.

"Son, fill her tank."

So, now me and my injured pride headed back out to the pump. When my tank was full, I picked up the nozzle and rather than hang it back up (which, you have no idea how bad I wanted to do), I knocked on her window.

"Ma'am, can you open your fuel door, I want to fill up your tank," I said.

She did, and I slid the nozzle in, and as my dollars poured into her car, I began to feel lighter.

I expected a cold, cool response or, maybe a polite, patronizing "Thank you." But this woman was beyond grateful. She had her granddaughter in the car and hadn't expected to need fuel when she left the house. She didn't know what she would have done without me.

God chuckled in my head all the while I finished filling her tank, and I got the opportunity to pray for her and her family. My night went from harried and bothered to cloud nine in a matter of minutes, all because of loving someone it made absolutely no sense for me to love in that way, at that time.

I have no idea what impact that may have had, but I'm guessing she paid that forward next chance she got, and that granddaughter will hear the story of Reckless Love from a God loving stranger repeated over and over, I hope it sinks in.
When you think about it, all of our Biblical examples fit this category too.

Jesus should never have even looked at the Samaritan woman. He had no obligation to her. She wasn't even fully

Jewish. She was considered unclean on so many levels, it broke the Pharisaical meter.

Legion was even worse. Here was a man unclean from living among the dead, infested with evil spirits and worthless in society's eyes, but Jesus didn't see that. He saw a soul worth saving.

And when Phillip took a look at the Eunuch, what did he see? Peter hadn't even had his vision, freeing them to minister to the Gentiles, and he was taking a huge chance. God honors us when we love those we can expect nothing from. It's all throughout Scripture.

Our second principle was an easy one as well. We can never overlook the value of just one person. Jesus hammered this point home, and God was constantly picking the one.

From Noah on down, the Bible is filled with examples of times God redeemed the world through the faithfulness of just one person, and reaching out to just one is no different.

No matter how many times I hear it said that ministry is not a numbers game, it's hard to remember sometimes. In human terms, numbers represent success. How many people responded? How many did you help with financial gifts? What was your reach, how many, how much, how big?

We give a lot of lip service to the idea that numbers are not what God is about, but when you select your youth camp speaker, be honest, given two equally charismatic speakers, and a similar cost, you're going to choose the one with the best batting average, am I right?

The reason this principle sticks with me, though, is that I've had it hammered home time after time.

One clear example occurred one night when I was slated to be the featured guest speaker at a huge youth event. I showed up early, set up my table with Why? cards and information and sat down to wait.

I assumed I'd be early in the program, but as the night progressed, I began to wonder. The crowd started to thin, and soon, it seemed like there was no point in my being there at all.

Finally, one of the organizers saw me and came over to apologize. "Oh, man, we didn't get you on the schedule for some reason. But we have a fifteen-minute slot right at the end, would you take it?"
I was ready to pack it in. In my head, I was already arranging my gear in the back of the truck and planning where to stop for food on the way home.

I was beaten down, but a tiny whisper in my head said, "Son, this isn't about you, it's for me, you need to stay."

So, instead of, "Yeah, you jacked up, bro! I can't believe I came out here, sat through all of this only to be ignored and now you have the nerve to ask me to squeeze my sermon into fifteen minutes, I was prepared for this!" I said, "Yeah, man, whatever you can do, don't sweat it, fifteen minutes is great!"

By the time I took the stage, that entire football field was nearly empty. I felt like the guys at the tech table were just waiting for the second hand to hit that magic hour so they could turn out the lights.

I launched into my abbreviated message, and I wasn't feeling it. Kids were walking away, talking out loud right in front of the stage and everything was wrong about this whole situation.

See, unlike Jesus, I didn't know there was a Legion in the crowd. Unlike Phillip, I didn't have the perspective of knowing what God could do.

Instead, I was kind of feeling like it was up to Kelly K, and this evening was going to bring my rep down, hard!

I finished up and offered an invitation, mostly because I always do. I didn't expect a response. But there, one young man stood in the middle of that field, surrounded by a sea of uncaring faces, one hand went up.

One person.

And even then, I was tempted to be ticked off. This should have been a dozen notches in my crown, at least! From a crowd this size? Shoot! Maybe two or three dozen, but one dude? He better be cool.

"Son," the voice in my heart said, "this was all about him. I sent you here for this one."

And at that moment, I felt so many emotions sweep over me. Humility and shame were first. How could I have pumped up my own ego so much to be wounded by this experience? Then shock.

God cared a lot about this kid to send me out here, glad I stayed. Then pure gratitude for the chance to pray with this kid and help him get his life on the right track.

Now, that night stands out, not as one of my greatest failures, but as one of my greatest successes, or should I say, one of God's greatest successes that He let me play a role in.

I wouldn't trade it. I learned a valuable lesson, and I'll never have the same reaction to that situation again. I say that now, but I'm sure I'll have to wrestle the demon of pride on occasion, but now I have some ammunition.

When I'm tempted to be disappointed about the size of a crowd, or a check, or the number of responses, I remember, this is not about me. It's about just one, each one, every time.

When it comes to just one, we never know what the ultimate outcome will be. The woman at the well was just one, but the three days Jesus spent in Samaria ended up revolutionizing an entire town with Reckless Love! He could have walked right on by her and taken his message directly to the masses, but he looked into her heart and saw the key to her friends and neighbors, a single heart changed by Reckless Love.

Legion was just one man, and Jesus had just left 5000. But here, in the darkness with death surrounding them on every side, light came. I told you we'd talk more about his impact and here it is. We don't hear anything else about Decapolis in the Bible, except for one thing. As Jesus made his way back home through Decapolis, in Mark 7, we find that the people have had a serious change of heart.

Where superstition and anger had been, there was a desire for the things of God. Scripture records that these same people who had run him out of their region now begged Him to stay and heal the sick.

So, what changed? We don't "know, " but I've got a pretty good idea.

That man, whose name used to be Legion, the one who begged Jesus to take him along, had happened. He'd gone back through the cities of Decapolis, sharing his story. Everyone in the region knew his "before" and when they saw his "after," it changed hearts and minds.

Once again Jesus saw a key, this time to an entire region. Remember, we mentioned before that Decapolis means "Ten Cities." The impact had reached an entire region.

So, what about the Eunuch? Phillip had just been preaching to crowds of admiring followers. People had even asked to buy the power they were displaying. It was some pretty heady stuff. He could have thrown up his hands at the idea of spending his day with this one, African stranger, but he knew better. He'd seen what Jesus had done with twelve men, and he knew what had happened in his own life after Jesus.

He clearly saw the power of one, so stepping into that chariot was a "no-brainer."

The results were remarkable.

Like I said before, we can't directly trace the roots of Ethiopian Orthodox Christianity to the preaching of this one man, but one thing is clear. Something changed in that nation. From the courts of Candice to today, it has been the cradle of faith in Christ. The earliest known Christian churches in the world, don't even date to Rome, but to Ethiopia, and I have to believe it all came down to one man being faithful to reach out to one stranger.

Now, on a continent that is still largely unreached with the gospel, Ethiopia has a thriving church of over 40 million believers. Not only that, but they also preserved some of the earliest known copies of the scriptures, all because of one man!

The third principle may be the hardest to grasp of any of the three, especially when, like Philip, you've already given up everything to do what you're already doing for Jesus. Be ready to be interrupted.

The most surprising things happen when you answer the call with "Here am I, send me" instead of, "I guess I could do that if there's no one else."

When I think of this, I think back to a night that really tested me. It was late. I was tired, and I wasn't feeling good. So, I got Jaxx,, my then infant son, to bed and showered, pulled on pajamas and crawled between the sheets. I was just about to drift off when my phone rang. I'd forgotten to pick up my daughter. Now, if you know me, the only thing more dangerous than interrupting me while I'm eating, is interrupting my sleep. I can handle almost anything with enough sleep, but without it, I don't even want to be around me, and it was about to get ugly.

I won't repeat what I muttered under my breath as I slammed around, getting the baby out of bed, collecting the other kids, and finding my keys. I managed to get my head on straight by the time I arrived to pick up my daughter, but I was not expecting the first thing out of her mouth. "I'm hungry!"

Of course, she was! Just perfect. Not only was I being interrupted, but now I was going to have to sit through the impossibly long line at Chick-Fil-A and pay too much for fast food! Great!

On the way there, I started thinking about my attitude and the example I was putting out for my kids, so I decided to engage in an act of Reckless Love when we got there.

I'll often pay the bill for a car behind me, and on this night, I really needed an attitude adjustment. So, I reached over and picked up a "Why?" card from a stack I keep in my car.

I decided to turn this into a teaching moment, the best way to get yourself out of a bad mood is to bless someone else. I knew this. "What do you say to we pay for the car behind us too?" I said, to my daughter.

The pretty little face in the passenger seat replied, "Yeah? What if their bill is like a hundred bucks?"

It was well after dinner, on a Thursday night, and I knew that in all likelihood, the vehicle behind me was just there for the awesome sweet tea anyway.

So, I grinned and shot back, "Well, then we'll pay a hundred bucks."

"Hi," I said at the window. "I'd like to pay for my order and the car behind me please, and would you give them this card and just tell them it came from the person who paid for their meal?"

"Sure, their meal comes to $5.67."

I'm pretty sure I stuck out my tongue in my daughter's direction as I paid and handed off the WHY card. But there was a problem. I gave the girl two cards, stuck together.

"Pay for the next car," the voice in my heart said.

"Why not?" I thought. "How bad could it be?"

"You know what, since there were two cards there, let's just go ahead and put the next one on that card too please?" "Okay," the cashier said, then her face sunk, "Are you sure about that? It's $57."

Laughter from the passenger seat.

It was at that moment a thought hit my mind while I was debating what to do. What if Jesus had looked at the cross and said, "No way! That's too much!" I'm really glad that's not what happened. That's the moment I realized, when it comes to Reckless Love, whatever the cost is, you pay it. And it should go without saying, I'm not just talking about money.

"Yeeeeaaah, I'm sure," I said, thinking through which bills might have to wait a couple of days. But, I knew, this interruption had happened for a reason.

Later that night, my wife saw a repost of a friend, of a friend, on Facebook, and there was a post with a picture of my "Why?" card.

"You'll never believe the day from hell I had, and then to top it off, we ended up having to buy dinner out, but the most amazing thing happened. When we got to the window, someone had left this card and paid for our whole order! I couldn't believe it! That was just what I needed! Thank you, whoever you are."

We just never know. Jesus takes a short cut through Samaria and interrupts His journey. He spends three days preaching and ends up back on track, exactly when He would have arrived taking a long way around.

Then, He interrupts a highly successful "camp meeting," with 5000 in attendance to run a boat through a storm and preach a revival of one in a graveyard, then goes right back to where He was.

Phillip walks away from his unfinished revival tour of Samaria, heads out into the desert to speak to an Ethiopian Eunuch, and ends up being ghosted to a new town, where he picks up as if nothing had happened.

In each of these cases, these slight interruptions in schedule led to great gains for the kingdom. One city, ten cities, and an entire nation were the gateways to a whole continent!

In my case, the one person who happened to receive that accidental second card, needed it, worse than I needed my sleep.

Reckless Love isn't something to engage in lightly. It's going to rock your world. It's going to force you to love those it makes no sense to love, it's going to teach you to never un-derestimate the value of just one soul, and it will most cer-tainly interrupt your busy schedule. But, I can guarantee, just like in all of these "case studies" we've taken a look at, it will more than make up for it in rewards.

So, we've unpacked this thing called Reckless Love and tak-en a good long look at what it is. If you're still with me on this, in the next section, I'm going to share with you some things we've learned on how to implement it.

And finally, in the last section of this book, I want to paint a picture of what I think this Reckless Love Revolution could mean for the future of the church and what we can accomplish.

So, if you're ready, let's move ahead. But, be sure you're prepared. I can tell you I wasn't. From here on out, things are never going to be the same for you or your world. If you really grab onto this, you're going to experience the most amazing things. Welcome to the Revolution.

CHAPTER 6
"Love Is Like A Bomb" - Def Leppard

We live in interesting times. While personal freedom on some issues is greater than ever, the ability to share deeply held convictions in a public forum has taken a beating. When it comes to Christian evangelism, we don't really have anyone to blame but ourselves.

In the past, the model was to seek out those we deemed most in need of Jesus, often identified by their low economic standing, and offer them a solution, with a catch. We'll clothe you, we'll feed you, we'll shelter you, but first, you need to get your ticket punched. Before we can share the compassion of Jesus, you'll need to get a full primer on the gospel. You're free to come and go, of course, but anyone who doesn't stay will leave empty-handed.

So, week after week, month after month, people who needed our help, subjected themselves to messages that were often more judgment than love, until Christianity became synonymous with a pious, hater attitude that most people grew tired of. As they rebelled, we doubled down. More fire and brimstone was obviously called for. In other corners, the gospel was swapped out for one that felt good but brought no real change and those that stepped into the world to fight the good fight, without understanding the price of discipleship, got their heads handed to them until they eventually gave up.

But, when you look at Jesus, neither of these modes of operating are present in his ministry. We see him befriending people and investing first, then lovingly revealing the truth. We often find him, rather than judging them, leaving the judgment up to them with the tough questions that led them to understand where they had gone wrong. But one thing was common throughout Jesus' ministry and the early church, wherever they showed up, Reckless Love was sure to follow.

It became their brand. When Jesus came to town, people got healed, addicts and the possessed got set free. The truth was spoken to power, and a new, refreshing view of a God that didn't hate them was revealed. Jesus himself often fed his listeners, and the early church continued meeting those needs, especially for widows and orphans who had no inheritance to support them. We see time and again, how those needs being met led people to faith.

So, why have we gotten so far off track?

How did a church founded by the man who met the woman at the well where she was with grace and compassion for humanity become a social agency that required a background check to get through the doors? How did the kingdom, built on the teachings of the man who freed Legion to a life of evangelizing Decapolis, become a dead-end stop for people who couldn't hack reality?

Something has gone horribly wrong with our faith. We spend time inventing new "heavy packs" to pile on men's shoulders without lifting a finger to help them. We've become professionals at white washing our own outward appearance to the world, while inside, we are decaying skeletons in so many cases. We've become a lot like the only people Jesus ever had anything harsh to say to. That must really break his heart.

That's not to say that we don't get some things right. We understand the urgency of the gospel, in some cases, and the value of a virtuous life. But the way we go about sharing it often reminds me of what Paul said to the young evangelist, Timothy, when he warned about those who have a form of godliness but deny the power of it. We give lip service to a God that can radically save and change us; then we continue to live unremarkable lives that are hardly distinguishable from those around us.

Of course, there are those that have made it their mission to be as different as possible from the "world" that surrounds them. But even this becomes more of an idol than anything if taken to its ultimate end. Rather than being known for the good they do for those around them, they become known for the "evil" they avoid. The piety they think to take on themselves can become a type of prideful judgmentalism for those who only see their lack of compassion for the outside world, mistaking it for condescension, instead of the protection they seek for themselves and their families.

How do we find a balance? How can we become a source of unconditional love to the world around us, and still have strong standards of virtue, morality, and ethics? Is it even possible?

We think it's not only possible, but we believe that is exactly the kind of love God is calling His people to in this time. We believe that unconditional, limitless love is exactly what the world needs and that's what we want to share with you. We believe that the same spirit that allowed Jesus to befriend harlots and tax collectors while maintaining his own purity is available and at work in us today.

When God first started speaking to me about this Reckless Love Revolution, he woke me up, literally and figuratively. So, here I am in the middle of the night with the words, "Love them," ringing in my head. "Love who, God?" was the best response I had at two in the morning. "Love them all," was his response. He began to talk to me about revolutionizing the way people love, and I began to see it differently.

Instead of leading with some big ask, I began to see that many of those we were trying to reach couldn't hear us.

Think about it.

Remember being a kid in school, when lunch time got close? It was hard to concentrate, and it's no different for those in need. As long as that need -- that desperation -- is screaming in their ears, they can't hear you. And even if they respond, it's more out of desperation than true faith. It's a good luck thing, maybe if I sit up straight and say amen, their God will notice me and take pity.

But, when you take the time to notice people, see them where they are and take note of their suffering and needs -- whatever they are, things change.

When you give a man with cold feet a pair of new shoes, suddenly, he has the bandwidth to listen to you. When you feed hungry people, their immediate need for survival becomes less, and they can see you. When you pray and see people healed, how can they not take the time to find out what you're about and why that happened?

Suddenly, the shoe is on the other foot. Instead of begging to get into their lives, or manipulating them into some half-hearted response to a message they barely heard, they are knocking down our door.

This is why wherever Jesus went, there were crowds. The good news preceded Him, and people showed up to see what was going to happen. Then, He'd teach them about a kingdom where they could be free and restored, and whole.

Surprisingly, He reserved his condemnation for the religious teachers of His day.

No one ever shows up voluntarily for a public tongue lashing, and He didn't hand out very many. But, too many times, as His followers, we tend toward the judgment, fearing the love is too weak to hold. We read His words, then gravitate toward one extreme or the other.

Truth without love, or love without truth. Both are useless. Instead of building relationships, we are out selling fire insurance, a good thing, to be sure, but it can't stop there. We are here for more than a rescue mission.

Jesus said His kingdom was among His disciples 2000 years ago, so where do we think it is now? While His message was about a kingdom not of this world, He founded it here to reach into eternity. We're called to help lay that foundation of living stones as souls are added to the kingdom, here and now.

One of my biggest frustrations with the institution of the church has got to be the Bus Stop Mentality. We share the Gospel to get people in. We punch their ticket. Then sit and wait for Jesus to come and pick us up and get us out of here.

I've got news for you, none of us know when He's coming.

Scripture is very clear on this. There are a lot of passages that say things like, "work for the night is coming when no one works," or "the fields are ripe for harvest, pray for God to send laborers" (John 9:4 and Matthew 9:38, respectively). It's very evident that while this earth is not our permanent home, we were to be about kingdom-work here as long as we are here!

But generations of Christians have spent their days just signing people up for a one-way ticket home, instead of affecting real change, right here and now in this world that He created for us.

That's what the Reckless Love Revolution is about. We are here and now, working to make changes in the world we see.

While it's easy to think we don't get to take anything with us, the most valuable "things" that surround us every day are ours for the taking. The people we meet and know and love - - the Bible says they are our inheritance, and we can take as many of them with us as we choose to.

By changing things here, we change eternity. It's the only interface we have. We've been placed here to learn and live the kingdom here and now.

While we know we were built for much more than what we currently experience, that doesn't excuse us from being fully engaged while we're on our journey. It makes no sense. If someone reached us, shouldn't our immediate response be to reach others?

Life on life and house to house is the clear pattern of the only generation of believers to reach the known world with the Gospel, in the 2000 years since Jesus left. And they managed it in a single generation.

That's why Jesus first word to His disciples when it came time for them to minister on their own was "go." He instructed them to cover the earth with the message of everything they had seen and heard and help others understand and believe it.

Why did He do that? Why would He have them spread this truth if there were no impact on the next life? Those who heard them preach the Gospel then became responsible for reacting to the truth they had learned. If there was no value for them in the next life, no repercussions for their sins, wouldn't it have made more sense for Him to ask them to remain silent?

After all, can a person truly be accountable for a truth they've never heard? Jesus thought so. There was an urgency to His message. He sent them out to preach a message of salvation and if we believe that, it should be our mission to do the same.

With over 55 million people stepping out of this world into the next every single day, shouldn't we be about sharing this message with every single one we can?

But we can't continue to do that in the same old way.

It's not working. In fact, the church in our day is shrinking.

People want compassion that makes sense. They want to see that we care about them as they are now. Not just as they will be. And we should care about them as they are now. It was Jesus' method of operation, and we are working hard to teach others how to bring that back.

Think about it, what other intimate advice about life would you feel confident in sharing with a total stranger? You wouldn't. It's like we understand this inherently in other areas, but somehow, when it comes to someone's eternity, we expect them to respect our opinion with no previous experience with us.

We tell them that God loves them, but we've shown no demonstration of that. There's no relationship for them to build trust on. Why would they believe us?

So far in this book, we've taken some time to define what we mean by Reckless Love and shown some pretty cool examples of it in scripture. Now it's time to start talking about how you can begin to overcome the bad stereotypes about your faith, build some really cool relationships, love on some awesome people and start to see some really cool results.

When you switch gears and start to really challenge yourself to physically share the love of God, things start to change.

As we move through this process, we're going to be referring back to our three main guiding principles. We want to reiterate the power of just one person, but now let's talk about the power of one person reaching out. We're going to talk about interruptions but in a different way. What if those interruptions, weren't really what they appear to be at all, but were part of God's design for us from the very beginning?

Finally, we want to clear up any misconceptions of who is eligible for Reckless Love. Just like anyone can be the target of it, anyone willing can be the delivery vehicle.
So, we'd like to challenge you to drop your preconceptions at the door.

We are about to share a new ministry paradigm that is going to be both easier like Jesus promised His yoke would be, and costlier, again, just as He promised, than anything you've ever ventured into before.

This isn't for cowards. I must warn you, that as you step into this and begin to really search out what it means for you, your family and your faith community to express Reckless

Love, you need to be prepared for God to slaughter some sacred cows and tear down some idols.

That's the thing about really seeking God, and not predefining where we'll find Him. He has a way of upsetting our well-laid plans and changing our perspectives.

So, if you're set in your ways, and ready to just hunker down in your bus stop and wait for the driver to show up on His white horse from the clouds, the rest of this book really isn't for you.

We understand.

The good news is, He loves you just the same, whether you follow us further into this adventure or not.

Now, to those of you who are reading this and you've just gotten more excited with every page and story we've shared so far, let me say the best is yet to come. We're about to share with you the strategies and tools we've been using to set Reckless Love Revolution in motion, and we've literally touched hundreds of thousands already, and we're just getting started!

But, I do have a warning for you too. If you think this is something you can just dip your toe into to see if you like it or not, you might want to have a seat with the bus stop bunch. It's not like that.

You see, as you begin to let God into your daily life, expect Him to show up and start doing things, He's going to challenge you. He's going to make you examine every relationship you have, every thought you think, every word you say. He's going to tap you on the shoulder at the most inconvenient times and ask you to do some radically stupid sounding stuff.

We could write a whole second book just on the silly stuff God has asked us to do in loving others, and we'll share some of it here, but don't say I didn't warn you. If you think you can try this for a day then just roll over and go back to sleep, it will haunt you. The love of God is not something you can play with, then just put away. It's an all-consuming fire, and it will wake you up and keep you up. It will cause you to give more than you ever thought possible. It will make you comfortable in the most uncomfortable of situations.

You see, Christianity is not a life style for lovers of comfort. Comfort zones are pretty, but nothing ever grows in them. This journey is going to stretch you to the breaking point, then show you the strength you never knew you had stretches even further. It's going to take your plans and blow them up because they're not big enough. It's going to shatter your idea of God, over and over and replace it with a clearer image as you get closer and closer to His heart.

In short, if you think Reckless Love Revolution is just about sharing something to change them, you might want to buckle up.

Everybody gets changed.

So, if you're ready to see things stirred up, walls broken down, eyes opened, your church changed forever, your community shaken from the ground up, and the spirit of the living God revealed in, through and around you, come on.

We can't guarantee you this will be safe, but we know it's fun. When we set out on this journey, we couldn't have ever imagined the places we'd go or the things we'd get to be a part of. We couldn't have predicted the awesome blessings we'd receive or the tremendous sacrifices we'd be asked to make.

But most importantly, we've come to a greater understanding of God and His love than we ever thought possible, and we're just barely scratching the surface.

Folks, our flight is about to take off, so settle back, buckle up and make sure your seat trays are locked in the full, upright position. No moving about the cabin until we turn off the fasten seatbelts signs when we reach cruising altitude. I want you to turn off your distractions and focus in, not on, what this book has to say to you. But to that still small voice, you may have gotten out of the habit of listening to, as you read these next few chapters.

As we take off and show you what it takes to put this into practice, we expect God will speak. As you read these next pages, you'll see things here we never knew were meant just for you, but He does. Pay attention. As you begin to get a clearer image of what it means to be a person, and a church that is committed to a Reckless Love Revolution, be prepared. You may be asked to change some things before we've even touched down. Remember, obedience is key.

We are praying for you, the readers of this book, regularly. We expect God to do great things with these ideas. We hope and pray that these ideas will not just encourage you to share in what we've seen. We hope you'll blow the doors off of that and set the bar even higher. As the author of Hebrews said, "Let us think of ways to motivate one another to acts of love and good works. And let us not neglect our meeting together, as some people do, but encourage one another, especially now that the day of his return is drawing near."

CHAPTER 7
"When It Came Down To Love, What Did You Expect"
- Richard Walters

In his first letter to the church, Peter uses a phrase that I love, "Now we live with great expectation." He's talking about Jesus' resurrection, and there's a lot of theology wrapped up in this passage that we don't need to unpack right now. But to me, the language here is some of the best in the Bible. It's bold. It's almost irreverent. And it makes a claim that challenges us to live beyond mere hope in the face of seemingly overwhelming odds.

See, in the resurrection, God demonstrated His complete dominance over creation by setting aside the rules of physics. He defeated the greatest power known to man -- death.

It's called the great equalizer. It's the thing we compare all other fears to, and the only way that we get to exit this life and move to the next. But we're told that Christ didn't just experience it, He beat it.

Not only that, but He's given us the power to beat it too. So, because of that, we live in great expectation.

This expectation, fueled by resurrection and based on the certainty of an inheritance we're told we couldn't screw up if we tried, is a forced to be reckoned with. It's the audacity to live beyond dreams, and mere "believing" launching us into the realm of faith, where the things we hope for become concrete.

Imagine the audacity Peter has here. He's telling us we don't just have the right to ask God to show up and do stuff. We are to live in the expectation of it.

When we ask God to love through us, we're to act as if it's already a done deal. We expect Him to show up and take what we bring and make something awesome out of it. And when we do, things have a tendency to take unexpected turns. But, when we don't, we often end up operating under our own power and living in disappointment much of the time.

Ironically, we then blame our inability to live up to His standards, when all the while, it was our lack of faith and lack of willingness to expect something amazing from God that prevented us from experiencing everything He has for us! And our expectations are contagious, too. Jesus even mentions it. There were times when an entire community refused to enter into expectation with Him and engage their faith to believe in healing. So, Scripture records they were able to stifle His ability to heal.

But, as we've discussed earlier, when the groundwork is properly laid, in the case of Samaria and Decapolis, expectations draw God's power like a lightning rod, and change happens.

This is something that God started talking to us about early on as we started on the Reckless Love journey. Whenever you decide to go out and do this, expect that God is going to show up and it's never a wasted moment. There will be times when the people's expectations are just not with you. They may reject your message, throw your WHY card in the nearest trash can and walk away. But your expectations shouldn't end there.

We're told that there are times when we are merely preparing the soil, then another plants, and yet another reaps a harvest. We have no idea what God's agenda in these cases are. We're to expect, and act in obedience wherever He sends us.

There was one Sunday that Ryan Hinckley and I were invited to preach at a church in Beverly Hills, California and we were stoked.

If you've never seen us in person, you might not get it when I say that we are polar opposites. I'm wide, and average height. Ryan is about six four, and skinny. He's the whitest guy I know, and me, I'm all tatted up and look like I might try and jump you in the parking lot. And who knows, I might! Just kidding. We look like a 21st-century version of Abbott and Costello, but not as funny.

It's not just our looks, though. We like everything different. It's rare we find a restaurant that makes both of us excited to eat there. He likes the hotel room warm; I like it cold. We like the driver's seat in different positions. We drink different soft drinks, eat different snacks, and root for different football teams. It's a match made in heaven.

But as a ministry team, we complement each other almost completely.

Ryan's strengths are my kryptonite and vice versa. I joke that I bring him along to make sure we sell some of our merchandise instead of giving all of it away for free and hitchhiking home.

When it comes time for ministry, he's very hands-on and quick to pray for people while I tend to hang back and say a lot of "Amens," to whatever he's saying (half of which I don't understand sometimes, because his vocabulary is twice the size of mine).

So, we walk into this church in Beverly Hills and immediately, we both felt God's presence.

We were greeted by the pastor and a group of people who were praying over the service for that day. And we know we're in Hollywood because the movie references start from the very beginning.

This guy sizes us up, and the first thing this dude says is, "Hey, you two look a lot like Timon and Pumba."

But, I didn't see it, because Ryan doesn't look like a warthog at all. But, I decided to let it slide.

When we preach, normally we tag team. One of us will start, and one of us will finish up. As I was finishing my part, I felt like I was supposed to do something I don't do that often and ask anyone who wanted to come up for prayer to meet us at the altar after the service.

It's a pretty upscale place, and I'm thinking, maybe a few of them will come down, then we'll get lunch, because warthogs work up an appetite preaching, and Timon was starting to look pretty good right about now.

But, that's not what happened.

Remember how I warned you not to even start this thing if you didn't want your life rearranged, well, this was one of those days.

As we wrapped up and I extended the invitation, to my dismay, I saw the rows emptying out into the aisles. But, unlike what I was expecting, no one was moving to the exits. Instead, they were all moving toward us!

I thought there must be some mistake, maybe there was an entrance up here I didn't know about, but it turned out, they all wanted prayer. So, I gave up my hopes of an early lunch and said, "All right, God, let's see what you have in store for us."

The first person in line was this beautiful girl, obviously athletic, but she was limping. Tears already flowing down her cheeks. We asked her to share. She told us she was there because she needed God to heal a torn Achilles tendon. She'd been told there's a chance it may never heal, and it was making it hard for her to walk. As if that was not enough, she went on to share that she was a professional ballerina and her doctors said there was a chance she might never dance professionally again.

No pressure.

Ryan, in his typical style, dropped down to his knees and laid hands on this girl's ankle. And in my usual style, I hung back and said a lot of "Amens" to everything he said. And it was good stuff, except I didn't catch it all because, in the back of my mind, I was arguing with God.

I wanted to play it cool, but I felt God say, "Ask this girl to walk to the back of the church and then tell you how it feels when she gets back." Right there in front of the entire congregation. But, I didn't wanna.

It's not just that this cramps my style, it's a risky move from my perspective. I was looking down this line and thinking,

"She's up here in the front, where everyone can see and if this goes wrong, this whole thing is going downhill from here."

Being late to lunch will be the highlight of my day because these people are all going to think we're a couple of amateurs! They might even start to doubt we know anything about what we're talking about at all, and I told God all of this.

"Ask her to walk to the back of the sanctuary and back, then ask her how it feels," He said again.

Meanwhile, Ryan is praying a great prayer.

"Can't you hear that, God? He's on fire. I can't interrupt that to say something stupid. Besides, surely what he's doing is enough. But, he's stopped to ask several times if she's felt anything with no results."

"Ask her..."

"All right!" and with a sigh, I look at this poor girl and say, "I think maybe, possibly, God wants you to try something. Could you walk to the back of the room and back here, and then tell us how it feels?"

She looked at me, hope in her eyes and nodded. Then she turned and began painfully limping back up the aisle. Every eye in the place followed her progress as she hobbled away from me and I started to look for the nearest exit.

I was not looking forward to explaining this, and just as I felt the crowd's gaze shift my way, she reached the back of the room.

By this time, my heart was about to thud out of my chest, and I was hoping I hadn't made a serious mistake, when she shouted, leaped into the air and sprinted back to the platform, completely healed.

The relief that flooded over me matched the grace that flooded that room for the remainder of our time there.

From the front of that line to the back, people started to receive answers. As each person came forward, God met them as I've never seen before or since.

It was nothing short of miraculous.

To top it off, several months later, when Ryan was in Chicago, who should he run into, but this ballerina. She was completely restored on that day and hadn't experienced a twinge of pain since.

The next day as we waited for our plane I sat, recapping our experience. I remember the conversation I had with God. I wanted some answers about what had happened that day. Not because it was something I didn't think He could do, but it struck me as odd that, all things being equal, it didn't always take place.

We'd been traveling that whole summer. Ryan and I were the same people we'd been the day before and the day after. It was in the same season in time. We'd even preached the same sermon, but experienced vastly different results.

In some places, people were healed and saved and miraculously set free, while in others, we could hardly get them to smile in church, let alone raise their hands in worship. And the few that came for prayer didn't seem to receive much at all. I wanted a simple answer to my question, "What was the difference?"

I remember hearing one word, "Expectation."

It had made all the difference.

Not only had Ryan and I showed up, expecting God to do things, not only had I listened and obeyed when prompted to extend an invitation, but the people had shown up expecting God to do amazing things too. Their expectations, coupled with our faith, opened the door to heaven on that occasion and as His word says He will, He poured out a blessing that was uncontainable.

God works with what we give Him. He's perfectly content to relate to us on our level. If all you expect when you go to worship is to high five some friends, listen to some good music, tweet a line from the pastor's sermon, and head out to lunch, He'll let you have it.

But if you expect more, He'll bring that too.

Show up with a thimble; he'll fill it. Show up with a swimming pool and the same Holy Spirit that fills your thimble without spilling a drop will fill that sucker to overflowing too! It's all the same to Him. We can't present Him with a challenge that is too difficult.

Expectation doesn't just work in church either. If we expect Him to, God will show up at work, school, wherever we expect to see Him.

But, we have to be ready to meet needs and share God. Don't expect God to show up unless you're ready to do your part. He may ask you to pray for people in the supermarket, share the Gospel in the dentist's office, or deliver a message to a 7-Eleven clerk. He'll show up if you expect Him to be there. Wherever you are, you just bring your humility and a willingness to serve.

This principle has become so real to me that I have started expecting God to show up everywhere I go. In fact, when I walk into new surroundings, the first thing I do is look and listen to see what He's going to do. It's gotten to where, when He gives me a break I'm disappointed. Reckless Love has become such a big part of who I am that expecting to engage in the miraculous has become my everyday reality and I wouldn't go back for anything.

My job is the best thing that's ever happened to me, short of being saved and maybe meeting my wife. Not a day goes by I'm not outwardly grateful for it, and I tell God all the time. It is truly amazing the things that happen when you find where you're supposed to be and step into the flow of God's spirit for your life.

As grateful as I am, I'm always aware that I could just as easily have missed it. God's no respecter of persons, and when He has a mission like Reckless Love, it's too important to risk it on just two guys. Ryan and I are so blessed to be a part of it, but I sometimes say a little prayer for the guys who didn't answer the call and I wonder, do they know what they missed?

As I've thought about this idea of living with great expectation, two things always jump out at me. First, when we live expecting something, we look for things we wouldn't otherwise. If I'm expecting a package from Amazon, which I love, I hear that UPS truck slowing down, I see that FedEx man pass my house and I wonder, did he miss me? The same is true with God, when our expectations are high, we're on high alert, and we're more apt to catch His clues when it comes time to jump into action.

Second, when we live in expectation, it builds our faith. We're almost disappointed when He doesn't speak. We know He will soon, and we can't wait. His stepping into our lives is no longer just a possibility. It becomes an inevitability. We know it's coming. We work as if good things are a certainty. We know they are coming. We don't just believe they might be.

On another occasion, I was outside an event at the merchandise table, which, next to teaching, is one of my favorite things about this gig. I always learn so much, which is even better. I've found that teenagers have a reputation for being loud and obnoxious, but are often shy and standoffish, especially in the beginning, and that was the case with a young lady who was pursuing my merch.

She dug through the shirts and looked over the table, coming back to one particular shirt. She held it up, and I could tell she really wanted to own it.

"How much is this shirt?" she asked me, hopefully.

There was obviously a price limit in mind.

"That one is twenty dollars," I told her.

Her face fell immediately, and she placed it back in the pile regretfully.

"Okay, thanks," she said, turning to walk away.

"Wait," I said, "What if God were to help you buy that shirt? What would it cost?"

She turned back, confusion squinching her face. "What do you mean?"

"Simple, if you were to ask God, right now, for help to pay for this shirt, how much would it cost?"

She turned back and sized me up like she was trying to determine if I was the good kind of crazy, or candy from a white van crazy.

I must have passed the test, because she said, "Fifteen?"

"Okay, for you, it's fifteen bucks," I said, handed her the shirt and accepted her neatly folded bills.

Her smile didn't stop at her face, it lifted her shoulders, and as she walked away, I could see it in her step, but then she stopped.

I could see the question coming from a mile away; it was the same one I would have asked.

She turned back, squinting suspiciously, "What if I'd said, $0?" she asked.

"Then it would have been $0!"

"Why?"

This kid was asking all the right questions. "Well, God works based on our expectations. When we expect Him to meet us all the way, He will. But, you only asked for a $5 discount, and you got what you expected," I said. "Next time, expect more."

She turned around, and as she walked away, I could see the battle waging in her mind between feeling great about her cool discount t-shirt, and feeling ripped off. Finally, the good feeling won, and she walked out of sight with a spring in her step. She'd gotten a bargain and hopefully learned a valuable lesson.

I hope next time she expects God to meet her more than part way.

The sad thing about this story is how divisive this idea is. I posted a video to social media of me retelling it, and it's gotten tons of views, but the thing that's most striking is the harsh comments it receives. I get called a heretic; have people tell me God's not about money; and that I should teach something besides some false prosperity doctrine. So, I've had to start following it up with my biblical reference (of course I have one. I try to make sure I can back up everything I teach with Scripture, the more, the better).

The story is recorded in 2 Kings. Elisha, the prophet, had taken on some ministry students, and just like ministry students now, they were broke. We know this because of what happened.

One of the men in his school passed away suddenly, leaving behind a wife and two children. Back in Elisha's day, being a woman was rough. You couldn't own property, or speak for yourself in legal matters. Being a widow was marginally better because there were legal requirements to set aside some funds for them, but the poor woman didn't know what to do.

She came to the prophet, "Elisha, you know my husband loved God and served faithfully, but now that he's gone, his loan has come due, and if I can't make this payment. I'm going to lose more than the furniture."

Back then it was common to use labor as collateral, and her sons had been put up as a guarantee and would be sold into indentured slavery for a time if she didn't pay.

But, Elisha didn't break a sweat. He'd hung out with Elijah during his own apprenticeship, and he knew what God was about. He expected God to meet this need, and he knew it didn't matter what the circumstances were.

"What do you have in your home?" he asked.

He knew whatever it was, God would show him how to get this woman what she needed.

"A tiny jar of oil is all we have left," she told him.

Then, Elijah taught her about expectations in a big way.

"Okay, go into your house and shut the door. Then, have your sons bring you every jar they can borrow from the neighbors. Get as many as you can. Do you hear me? Don't just stop with a few jars; God wants to take care of all of this. As soon as you fill one jar, set it aside and keep pouring. Don't stop until you've filled them all."

I'm sure this woman must have given Elisha that same look the t-shirt girl gave me at my merch table. He was definitely crazy, but was it good crazy? But, she trusted him. After all, her husband had sought him out to get trained in prophetic ministry, so she took her sons and went home.

Can you imagine gathering those jars, "What's it for?"

"Uh, the prophet asked me to get them."

There were eye rolls at this point, I'm sure.
"Oh, one of those kind of things, sure, Abram! Bring the widow a couple of those empty wine jars, no not the good ones. It's for an Elisha project. Last time he smashed one..."

Then, she lined them up on her kitchen floor, and it was her kid's turn to give the crazy taste. Mom had lost her marbles.

Imagine it. Your mom has this tiny jar in her kitchen, where she keeps the olive oil. It maybe holds a cup or two, so she sends you out to gather up five-gallon buckets and line them up on the kitchen floor.

"Mom, what are you doing?"

"Elisha said to fill these buckets with this oil," your mom says, with a wild look in her eye.

"Seriously? Mom, do I need to call grandma again? Did you take your meds?"

But then, she starts pouring and pouring and pouring. By the time she's had you carry the fifth bucket to the garage, you're starting to get interested.

"What are you going to do with all of this? Mom, isn't that enough? Seriously, this is slave labor."

"No, honey, slave labor is what will happen to you and your brother if this doesn't work, be quiet, I'm trying to concentrate. I don't want to spill any."

So, the widow fills her jars, "Okay, bring me one more."

"We're out of jars mom."

"Did you look?"

Eye rolls, "Gah, mom, yes, I looked!"

"Are you sure, because the last time you said you looked there were three more in the hall," and like moms everywhere for all time, she goes to check for herself.

"I swear, I have to do everything myself around here. I don't really even know why I'm going to the trouble; it would be so much easier not taking care of your...huh, well, I guess you were right this time."

The Bible tells us that she went to Elisha, and they took inventory. Not only was there enough oil to cover all of the debt, but Elisha instructed the widow to save the rest to live on.

God didn't just meet her immediate need; He funded this woman's retirement!

When it comes to loving others, God is not stingy. Ask big. Expect more. When your big expectations become inevitable, your faith can move mountains. So, don't think you're expecting too much. Figure out what you need, ask for what you want, then make sure you've got plenty of jars. Your God wants to meet you all the way in this Reckless Love Revolution.

CHAPTER 8
Paying The Price Of Love
- The Bee Gees

"We can never out-give God," or so goes a phrase I heard throughout my growing up years. The sentiment behind it is so true. Our God is overly generous with us. In fact, we've found God meeting needs before we even knew we had them on this journey. But, there is a flip side to almost every coin when it comes to serving God. While He doesn't keep score or demand we perform to be blessed; He does ask us to join Him as partners in ministry and give into other's lives out of the abundance He gives to us. Sometimes those asks are small and easy, but sometimes they're painful.

That's why, when we work with groups on starting their own Reckless Love Revolution, we cannot stress enough that you must be ready to pay the price. When you step out in faith with big expectations, sometimes God makes the oil you have fill all of your jars. But sometimes, He presents you with trucks filled with olives and an oil press and He asks you to help Him make more. You don't get to pick and choose how this works. It's His revolution and He sets the agenda.

If you've ever been on any kind of foreign mission trip, as part of your briefing, they probably told you, "Don't bring anything with you that you are unwilling to give away."

It's true. As the people you minister to steal your heart, you will be moved to bless them in big and small ways, and you'll find yourself giving the clothes off of your back, and the shoes off of your feet. But, I don't really feel this principle goes near far enough.

In my own life, growing up and right up until today, in times when I've been consciously walking with God, my own standard is a little higher. I never own anything I'm not willing to give away. Everything I have, right up to the big stuff is at His disposal. He's not asked me to give away my car or home yet, but they belong to Him anyway, and I have no business claiming to represent Him as a minister of His love, unless I'm prepared to sacrifice whatever is called for.

We love because He first loved us.

Scripture tells us that love is defined by this: while we were still completely oblivious to our sin and in active rebellion against God, Jesus submitted Himself to be executed to pay the cost of our bad choices and wrong behaviors.
The bar is set pretty high.

Even Abraham was given a reprieve when he was asked to sacrifice his son Isaac, but our God is not one to ask anything of us He'd not willingly do. To prove it, He made the ultimate sacrifice, in allowing His own creation to take the life of His son.

So, any time I'm tempted to balk at what God asks me to give away, the cross looms before me and my excuses melt away.

That's not to say I'm perfect. I'm just consciously aware that no matter how much I may give up to serve Him, I can never come close to equaling the price He was willing to pay to redeem me. Even before I knew Him. He was willing to pay the price, and Reckless Love requires us to be willing to give whatever it takes to meet needs and reach people for Jesus.

That was never more true than just recently. This ministry has taken off and grown more quickly than I could ever have imagined. Even in just a short time, the opportunities we have today are tremendous. We are asked to speak in churches, camps and conferences across the nation.

One of those opportunities was being a part of a recent conference. It was an honor to be asked.

Since the conference was just getting started, their budget was somewhat limited. They asked participants to help provide some of the things they would need to make the experience everything they wanted it to be. They requested that I find a laptop suitable for serving up the video and slides for the various presenters throughout the conference.

I'm pretty good with tech, so I said, "No problem," and put out the word.
We were getting down to the wire and about a week before the conference, we still didn't have what we needed. So, I spent some extra time in prayer over this issue, laying out my expectations before the Father.

It wasn't long after that a gift arrived from a woman who had an extra laptop and wanted to see it put to a good use. We thanked Him for his provision, and I got busy setting up the software. There was only one problem. The machine, although it worked well for what it was, was too outdated to run the required program. We were right back where we started.

In those moments, it's tough to maintain your expectations. I knew God had given us what we'd asked for, but it wasn't quite right, so it seemed like there should be more. I wasn't ungrateful for what we'd received. It was a very generous gift and I'm sure we'll find the perfect use for it, but it just didn't quite fill our need. Time was running out.

I understand this situation well, because I use my laptop a lot for school and sermon writing, along with business and a million other things. The one I had was beginning to show its age as well. We just continued putting this need before God and expected Him to show up. It's amazing what happens when you don't let the first sign of discouragement slow you down, or make you change course.

It wouldn't have been the end of the world. Worst-case scenario, we would find a machine to use, but I'd told them I'd find one. And the truth was, I felt a bit like a failure for not being able to come up with such a simple donation.

You never know when God is preparing something for you way down the road. It might be money or a relationship. It might be a skill you learn that you think you're never in a million years going to need. There's something about having the long view that is so amazing. From where God is, He sees the beginning and the end. He's able to map out His agenda for us over time and space in ways we can't even begin to understand.

I've pretty much started to just accept odd things when they show up. Even if I don't need it somewhere down the line, someone else will.

In this case, it was a relationship with a dude in Midland, Texas who I hadn't seen in years. In fact, I hadn't thought about him much at all, and over time we'd lost touch. Just as we were coming down to the wire, he messaged me to say he'd been following my progress into ministry and he wanted to do something for me. He knew I needed a new Mac Book to keep up with all of my various tasks and he was willing to buy it for me, brand new. All I had to do was go to BestBuy near my house and pick the sucker up.

Somewhere, in the mind of God, there was this moment, waiting for this connection to make sense again. If I tried to map out all of the "coincidences" and wrong turns that turn out to be divine intervention, I could spend the rest of my life and still miss many of the details. Through years of separation and no communication. God had somehow kept this connection alive enough to turn it back on at this moment, just when it was needed.

To say I was excited would be a total understatement.

I love new toys and walking out of BestBuy, all I could think of was getting home, opening up this box and setting it up the way I like it. I thought about what I needed to transfer my files, and how much nicer it would be to have a machine that wasn't constantly lagging, or feeling like it could shut off at any moment and never turn back on. The time I would save could be put to better use in ministry, or spent with family, and this was a big chunk of money I now wouldn't need to spend in the near future.

The conference was benefitting too. With my files stripped off and the computer reset, my old computer could easily run the software required to meet all of the needs of the conference. In fact, it was way more than they needed and I felt generous calling them up the night before to let them know about this generous gift I'd been given. They, in turn, were excited to hear that the need had been met.

But, I just couldn't do it.

That night I sat there, gazing longingly at that box, but something inside me told me, it wasn't mine to keep.

Then there was that voice challenging me, "Kelly, you're a good giver."

"Well, thanks, God."

"When it comes to giving away what you don't need."

Ouch.

Somehow He always knows exactly where to strike to get right to the heart of the matter.

God went on, "But, can you give away something you don't just need, but you really, really want?"

It was like dangling cake in front of a fat kid. All the way home, I'd envisioned that shiny new case. I'd pictured it on my desk, the new keys gliding smoothly under my fingers, all the awesome sermons we'd write together. Now that dream had died before it had even been removed from the package.

But, I knew it was the right thing to do.

The conference had asked me to provide them with a computer, and in my mind, I was giving this to God, how could I give Him less than my best?

There's a story in 2 Samuel where my man David is in a jam. There's a plague coming, and he's worried that it will wipe out many of his subjects. So, Gad comes to David and tells him, "Go to Araunah's threshing floor and offer a sacrifice so that God will spare the people."

David has plenty of experience with both obedience, and disobedience by this point and he knows better than to test God. So he goes.

When he gets there, this farmer, Araunah, the Jebusite, sees him coming.

"Hey King, what can I do for you?"

So, David explains his predicament and this dude, who doesn't even worship Yahweh, the God of Israel, is down with all of it.

He starts by giving David the threshing floor, and he even throws in some oxen for a sacrifice and his own wood farming implements to build a fire with. He is all in. But David hesitates. See, he was beginning to understand how to relate to God, and he knew what a sacrifice meant. It required giving something up and as tempting as this offer was, he knew it wasn't going to cut it.

"Sorry, that's a very generous offer, but I'm afraid I'll have to pay for all of it, so total it up, and I'll pay what's fair."

"No, really, it's my pleasure. It's the least I could do. Hopefully, your God will hear you and honor your sacrifice, but I can't take your money. I wouldn't feel right making a profit from this."

"I understand, Araunah, you're making a noble gesture, but what good is a sacrifice that doesn't require anything of me? How can I offer to God what costs me nothing."

In hindsight, this passage fits this situation so well that it should have come to me, but all I could think of was all that glittery Mac goodness just sitting there, waiting to be taken advantage of and here I was in need of just such a device.

The blessing was mine. He had, after all, given the computer to me. And it wasn't like my offer wasn't generous. I could have sold my old machine. Even in its current condition, it was worth $500 easily. Do you know how far that gets you on the road? That's a round trip air fare or 20 tanks of gas.

Did I mention I can use all the funding I can get?

But somewhere in the back of my mind, God's voice kept re-playing, "How will you do if I ask you to give up something you really care about?"

I'd done it before if you recall.

Somewhere, there was a dude riding buses with my Raider's jacket on, after all. I was a generous guy. The choice was mine, and I think God would have blessed me either way.

There are times when he gives us a test, and it's pass/fail. Then, there are those tests that just unlock new achieve-ments. This wasn't life or death, but I knew what I had to do, so I called the conference.

It was a hard call to make because I knew I couldn't just drop this computer in their laps without explaining. I was ashamed. Even though it had been perfectly within my rights to keep that glorious new piece of technology, something in-side of me was repulsed by how greedy I had been.

If I have to guess, it was my mother's voice, echoing through the years that tipped the scales and made me realize what I needed to do.

In Luke Chapter 14, Jesus presented the challenge to follow Him. First, He states that anyone who wants to follow Him must take up their cross and follow. There is a cost to this discipleship thing that must be paid from the very beginning. He compared it to a man building a tower who will count his wealth to see if he can complete it, for fear others will see his unfinished tower and mock him.

Before we can set out to love in radical ways, we need to weigh the expense. While this may occasionally be financial, that's not my primary concern. Money is an easy thing to come by when God is behind what you're doing. I'm talking about the cost in time, emotions and effort that you'll have to put out just to make contact with the world around you. Then, there are the continued costs of maintaining those relationships once they are entered into. Are you ready to love the people God puts on your heart, not just one time, on one day, in one way, but until He tells you to stop? Even when it gets messy, time-consuming and threatens to spill over into the rest of your life?

You see, if we're going to get away from the bus stop mentality, it's not enough to follow the old way. We can't just go out into the streets and drag them in. Many of them simply won't go, and it was never the right approach, to begin with. We've got to meet them where they are, wherever they are, in whatever they're in. We've got to be prepared to get our hands dirty to help them. This is how we win their hearts so that we can introduce them to the one who holds ours.

We're no longer dealing with our grandparents "lost" who once sat in Sunday School and spoke our language, even if they're a bit rusty. Many of the people we reach out to today have never seen the inside of a church building. Others are actively opposed and resistant to anything having to do with "religion" after being hurt and abused by it.

Before we can talk to them about changing, we need to show them that we care about them now, warts and all. And the cost can be tremendous.

Another warning from Jesus says, "If you set your hand to the plow and you look back, you're not the right kind of worker for the kingdom." (Luke 9:62)

We've got to be in this for the long haul. It may not always be a weekend project, then back to church as usual. In fact, if God interrupts you, as we'll talk about more here in a minute, it won't be. The broken and hurting will come, but that has its costs too. It may cost you members, as they reject the very people you are ministering to. It may cost you your programs, your agenda, and even cause you to redirect your budget from what felt important to things God calls you to.

It's easy to romanticize sacrifice. Standing boldly with the poor and living a stark life to give all you have to them. But, God knows where you live, and He will ask you to sacrifice things, even things you need. Good things. Important things. All for the sake of the kingdom. Jesus wasn't fooling around in the passage following the parable of the tower when He says that anyone who will not give up everything to follow Him isn't right for the job.

But, it's not just about the sacrifice, or putting others first. In combat, a unit cannot survive if a soldier's head is not fully "in the game." And we can't either. If there is anything the enemy can distract you with, anything that has a bit of your heart that's not wrapped up in who He is, it will become a problem at the most inconvenient time. So, am I making the challenge that Jesus made to the rich young ruler?

No, not for most of you. Some of you may need to sell everything, but that's not what I'm saying.

In order to be wholly committed to the work of revolutionizing the way you love, and making that contagious, you can't be half in. Some of you are about to close this book right now. You don't feel called to full-time ministry. You may think you can't engage in Reckless Love because you only have five minutes. You may think you're not eligible because you've only got $2.

But, remember, the widow's pennies? Remember the brief conversation that Jesus held with the Samaritan Woman? All God is asking for is all of what you have and nothing you don't.

If you've got five minutes to spare from your busy family life, use it wisely and engage. Be in the moment with those God shows you to love.

If you've got $2 to give, be intentional and meet the biggest need you can meet with that $2.

The same God that filled the widow's oil jars will meet you where you are, even in your need, and bless your gift. But, it's got to be given with an open hand, and a committed heart.

It's important when the Reckless Love Revolution begins to spread beyond you personally that you share this message with everyone in your community. They need to understand what this means. Reckless Love cannot be given grudgingly or expecting something in return. It's not a one time gift we don't have to think about again, and before we commit to building this tower, we need to make certain we are willing to pay the cost. What He wants is our willing obedience, and He will supply the rest.

CHAPTER 9
"And If You Got One, Love One"
- Common Market

When I think back through people we've ministered to on this crazy ride we're on, I don't see a crowd. I don't see a city; I don't even see churches. I see individual faces. I think of people whose lives had been turned upside down being righted, and I remember to never underestimate the power of one life.

I think back to that football field and that one hand going up, but there's more to this power of one thing than that. Before we can effectively engage in a Reckless Love Revolution, we've got to turn that concept around and recognize the power of one to reach those souls who are lost and hurting.

Sometimes, it's easier to hear God tell me who I'm supposed to pray for, or give to than it is for me to hear Him telling me, "Good job son."

It's easy to forget, as close as we all are to our own mistakes, that we are the catalyst God uses to reach out to broken people. Even if you are the only one, you can make a huge difference.

I could write an entire book about how God has used me, a former insult comic, with too many tattoos to count, to challenge people's perceptions of who He is. And I love the irony that most of my ministry is not to people who look like me, and are outside of church, but it's speaking truth to power. It's challenging leaders to step out and take their people with them. It's engaging Christian youth to move beyond the four walls of the church.

I'm sure Ryan feels the same. His background makes him uniquely unqualified to speak anything to pastors and elders and youth leaders in the mainstream Christian church. We feel a lot like Paul in some ways.

But, when God spoke to me and said, "Love them, love them all, I want you to revolutionize the way people love," I was the only one there.

When Ryan heard a similar message, it was a solitary experience for him too.
In fact, in Scripture, when Jesus calls people, you'll notice, it's not in groups or families.

It's one on one.

But, it's easy to think you've got to have a revolution to start a revolution. That's not the way it works. While revolutions are won by armies, they are nearly always started by one voice that revolts against the status quo.

They start when a young attorney stands up in a rural church and instead of talking about appeasing the Brits, he preaches a rousing sermon that ends with, "Give me liberty or give me death."

They start when one unassuming little man in India begins to teach people to be the change they want to see in the world.

Just as every forest starts with a single seed, and every forest fire with a single spark, one person, truly expecting God to show up and change things through Reckless Love, and ready to pay the price, can be the voice that changes everything in a community. And that community can influence a state, then a nation, then the world.

When Jesus spoke to a single woman, she, in turn, became the voice that gathered Samaria to hear His message. From whore to spokeswoman for God in a day is a pretty dramatic transformation. Once she understood that what Jesus offered was unconditional, Reckless Love, her expectations were ignited, and she was willing to face the potential ridicule of her own people to share that love with others.

Because of Jesus taking the time to speak into one life, an entire city was changed, and later we find Phillip welcomed when he came to Samaria to share this same good news. I wonder, how many of those who believed Phillip's teaching had seeds planted by this Samaritan woman and her story of the Messiah's kindness to her?

If the apostles could have written a list of the most likely prospects for teaching the Gospel, I doubt that a crazed, demon possessed lunatic in the graves of Decapolis would have made the top ten. But once that one person had been changed, the power of God moved through him to reach the ten cities of Decapolis. Can you imagine, if you'd gone through the streets of Decapolis the day before, proclaiming that Legion was coming and he was bringing news of the Messiah with him, the reaction you'd have gotten?

They probably would have fitted you with chains and parked you next to him, diagnosing you as a mad man.

But, God didn't care.

Even after all of the people of Decapolis, except for this one man, rejected Jesus.

Even after Legion's miraculous recovery, one man was enough to change things.

When Jesus returned, He wasn't just greeted warmly, but the truth had spread by the word of this one man until the men of the cities came out and begged Him to stay and heal the sick.

All because of one man.

A Eunuch was about as unlikely a suspect as could be imagined when it came to spreading new ideas. After all, how could he make a lasting impact, with no way to reproduce? He was truly solo. A man's children, in that time, were his legacy. But yet, if that had been all that was stacked against Phillip's friend, the results would be remarkable. Even though he was a member of the royal court, not only would he never have a family, but the man was a servant. Why would anyone take notice of him?

We have records of two other young men who shook Empires while wearing the chains of servitude in both Joseph and Daniel. I wonder, was our Ethiopian friend cut from the same cloth?

While we can't mark the direct connection, I fail to believe that it's any coincidence that from this one interaction, grew an entire nation of over forty-two million believers that exists to this very day as one of the birthplaces of the church.

All throughout Scripture, we are shown this model. When God seeks to shake things up, He speaks to individuals, not nations. Noah, Abraham, Moses, Samuel, David, Nehemiah, were critical in the establishment and preservation of the nation of Israel, yet each started from a position of no great influence. It was based solely on their expectations, and willing obedience rose to change their worlds.

Just in case you think God leaves the women out, Deborah, Esther, Ruth, Rahab, Miriam, and even Jesus' own mother, Mary, were mighty women used by God to carry out His plan. Without even the equal footing of being a man, these women influenced nations and even the whole world through Reckless Love and a willingness to pay the price to achieve what God was calling them to.

As you look down through the ages, a pattern seems to emerge, and it's this: God honors relationships.

From the beginning of time until now, he has selected and worked through men and women who would listen to His voice and obey. But He didn't reveal His plans, for the most part, in a congregational setting. But, in private conversation with a single person. Step by step, His plan is unfolding to bring us back into harmony with Him, until we relate to Him face to face one day in eternity, just as Adam did in the garden.

I think we often spend so much time thinking about the church as a whole and how we fit into it, that we forget it is designed to bring individuals to the Father, through Jesus. There is a tremendous power in the individual that cannot be wielded by a crowd, or an army. A crowd may shout you down, or coerce you into action. An army may bring brute force, threaten, and even kill, but only an individual has the power to speak, one to one, into another human soul. One heart to another is the only way that life change actually takes place.

Not only that, but mobs and armies are raised by the voice of one person standing up and convincing others to join them in their cause.

When God spoke to me about starting this ministry, at first, all I could see was everyone, everywhere. It was almost as if I was getting that view you've seen in a comedy, where the camera pulls back, and back, and back until you're looking at the whole world from space, before being plunged back into the action.

It seemed ginormous.

I couldn't do it, and I told Him it was too big, but I knew that He was talking to me, and somewhere, something inside me was answering because in my heart I knew. He doesn't call us to do things we can't do.

So, some of you are asking right now, what can one person do? The excuses begin to come.

"I'm young."

"I need help."

"I'm not a 'leader.'"

"No one will listen to me."

"I'm too old, too weak, too worthless."

Here's the thing, all God is wanting is relationship, and if you're reading this book, you've got the ability to relate to Him.

I don't care if you're paralyzed from the nose down, stuck in a giant wheel chair, and can't afford the fancy speaking gear that gives guys like Steven Hawking a voice, you have a mind.

You can pray. That prayer can move others to act.

Let me tell you what I mean.

When I first responded to this call that I had been running away from since I was thirteen, no one would let me into their church, hardly, let alone let me preach. But, I knew God was speaking. So, I did what I know to do. I went around the gate keepers and went straight to the audience. I started talking to myself, well, to a camera, really.

I knew I was supposed to preach and if I couldn't get in front of a crowd, I'd make my own.

If there is one thing I've learned to do, its stir people up, and I'm not afraid of controversy.

So, I started talking about topics that most preachers can't, and it started to work.

On YouTube, it went okay, but when I started sharing stuff to Facebook, it took off. I was getting comments, people were watching and sharing my stuff, and the word was starting to get out. All because of the power of one person. I was just me, with my camera and my computer.

It doesn't take money, or an organization, or community, or a church to begin loving people. One person, expecting God to show up and do what He's going to do somewhere, anyway, and being willing to give whatever they've got to pay the price, can change everything.

Even if that one person is you.

Here's an analogy that many will find amusing, but, I think it fits.

Have you ever been approached by someone who wants to talk to you about a "business opportunity?" They start showing you proof of what others have done with this business. They call it "the business" as in, "people in the business..." but they won't really say what's going on? First of all, run. No, but seriously, they are getting your curiosity up about this amazing thing. Then comes the plan. Whether they sketch it out on paper, or, they've made enough sales of whatever miracle product it is, to buy a white board, it all starts the same. They draw a circle, and in this circle, they write one word, "You."

Then, they begin to describe how you, with a small investment, can start from zero and by influencing just two friends to join you, can begin to build your own business, with a small commission from each of these people for their use and sales of the products that could lead to millions of dollars!

If you've never been approached by a network marketing person before, this can be overwhelming. They all have the numbers to back it up, and all of their products, according to them, are miracle workers, but I'm not interested in any of that. No matter what company it is, or what they are selling, they all start with one three letter word, "You."

One person, reaching two people, who each reach two people, who each reach two people is eleven people. At the next level, it's thirty-three, then ninety-nine, you get the picture.

One person, loving Recklessly, becomes three, then seven, and before you know it, you need a bigger building to hold them when you get ready to launch your next campaign.

What God began to show me, when I was tempted to pull out to that global view and feel overwhelmed, was faces. One person here, one person there, two over here. And eventually, it began to sink in.

I was just one person, but, I could start from where I was, with what I had, to do what I could do and see what happened.

It worked.

Before I knew it, people were getting excited about my stories, my family and friends were joining in, and now literally millions have heard me speak and seen my videos around the world.

But, I was alone when it all started.

Now, here's the really cool part, I didn't even have to figure any of it out. It came to me. I stepped out, expecting God to show up, willing to give what I had and He began to show me who to love.

Now, it's an everyday thing. Everywhere I go, I'm no longer just me. When I'm reaching out to that one person God shows me, I know that somewhere, Ryan is doing the same. I know that somewhere else, my awesome mother, Echo, is doing the same and now I know, that many of you reading this book are going to join me.
Because that's how it works.

From me in my living room, feeling overwhelmed, my reach began to multiply, until I was no longer begging for a place to preach every week, I was begging for a day off.

As people catch hold of this vision, they get involved. It's simple, it's easy, it's effective and God is in it, but it has to start with just one person, and today, that person is you.

So, take stock, because now that you've read this, the Holy Spirit is coming for you. Wherever you go, He's going to begin nudging you. But, He won't force you to join Him, He's not like that. He knows that voluntary followers are the only truly genuine force He can use to reach the world.

When we choose to obey, our will becomes entangled in His, and something awesome happens. We get to help Him in this great restoration project He's about, calling His creation back to Himself.

Here's the thing I realized. Once I started practicing Reckless Love, it no longer mattered to me that I was alone, because I wasn't. I was surrounded by grateful people, some of them were starting to reach out to others, and I was having so much fun that it stopped looking like work and became an obsession.

Remember I said I have to take Ryan to keep from giving away all my merchandise? I love loving people.

As momentum begins to build for you from your very first experience, you are going to find out that you get so much more back from this, and you won't be alone for long.

See, when Jesus starts moving on people, they get excited, and they can't help but tell others. Just like Legion and the woman at the well, you'll be sharing with everyone who will sit still to listen to the awesome experiences you're having. You'll start to feel like you're bragging after a while because life gets that good.

The truth is, the idea that one person isn't enough to start this is kind of a smoke screen, for one simple reason. The truth is magnetic.

When you start to live it out loud, without judgment, without making demands on people they are not ready to be part of; people are drawn to it.

Once you've taken your first few steps, you'll understand that worrying about whether you can do this on your own is really silly. The truth is, you won't be on your own for more than a few minutes.

Not to be sappy, but I need to make one other point here before we move on to other things. As believers, our fear of starting things alone is truly a lie. When Jesus said He would be with us to the end of this age, it wasn't just a metaphor.

As you begin to move into active service in this Reckless Love Revolution army, you'll find His presence is more real than you've ever experienced it. It's impossible to share the love of God, without it first passing through, and affecting us, and the results are amazing.

So, the next time you start to feel like you can't do this, find a mirror, look yourself in the eye, remind yourself you're not alone and that all you have to do is this one thing, obey. With each action you take, you'll find it gets easier until your resistance is gone and you feel compelled to engage in acts of Reckless Love everywhere you go.

Don't let your enemy get the best of you. Sometimes the only weapon he's got is stopping us before we ever get started.

Jesus said that He was going to the cross because of the prize set before Him. That prize was you. Remember that, then set your eyes on those He's calling you to impact and begin to see them as your prize.

It's amazing what can happen when one person, expecting God to show up and do amazing things, is willing to act in reckless obedience to recklessly love just one, then one more.

CHAPTER 10
"The Power Of Love Is A Curious Thing"
- Huey Lewis and the News

When God sets out to work through us, it's a bit of a "dumbing down" process for Him. We write volumes on how He works, and we list all of the things we believe we know about Him, but the truth is, there are not enough books in this world to adequately describe His infinite nature. He spent some time explaining it to Isaiah.

"I don't think like you think, and I don't do things the way you would do them. Look up. See how high the heavens stretch above the earth? Can you reach it? No. That's how far apart the way I think and work is from your own thoughts and deeds. When the rain falls from heaven and waters the earth, do you see how it brings new growth? It produces enough that the farmer can plant a new crop, and the baker can still have flour for bread. When I say something, it doesn't just echo back to me like your voice does. No. Everything I say goes out and accomplishes what I set out to do, before it returns."

That's a big difference between our agenda and His.

From His perspective, things look a lot different than they do from street level. That's why when God expresses His agenda, it can sometimes feel like a slap in the face. Here we are, doing good things, when He comes along and asks us to stop and move on to something else. It's easy to let your pride enter in and try to convince Him that you need to finish what you're doing first.

Phillip could have argued with God. He was preaching a great revival in a place that really needed it. He could have stayed right where he was and no doubt, God would have moved. But, he'd learn to expect God's voice, and he knew that whatever God was about was where he wanted to be.

That's why he immediately stopped preaching, packed up and started walking to the desert road. Somehow, he took the interruption in stride, but he didn't have to.

One thing I've learned about God is that He won't drag you away from it. You're welcome to stay and try to make it work on your own, or you can move in obedience. The choice is always yours. But, I've also learned something else. I need to be ready for interruptions.

We discussed this in the first part of the book, the woman at the well, Legion, and the Eunuch were all interruptions from the course Jesus and Phillip were on. But were they really? I have my doubts.

If there was ever a time for my agenda to be lined up with God's, you would think it would be in the middle of a sermon, but even then, sometimes, God interferes. As a former pro-fessional performer, I take my preparations seriously. Not to draw to close a parallel between preaching and being a standup comedian, but for me, writing a sermon uses the same mental muscles as writing a comedy routine.

Ask anyone who's ever stepped to the mic to tell jokes in front of a crowd, and they will confirm what I'm about to say. Once you get up the nerve to do it, and you've started into your patter, the last thing you want is an interruption at an inopportune moment.

Preachers have one big advantage. Interrupting them is not only a frustration for them, but it's also an established taboo. It rarely happens, but leave it to kids to not understand the important rules we grown-ups have established for access-ing God's message.

One Sunday, I was serving as guest speaker for a congrega-tion, and I'd brought my A game. I was well into my sermon when a young man in the audience caught my eye. He'd been eyeballing me for a little while, and I could see he was thinking about something that was leading to a question, but, since that's a nearly unforgivable breach of protocol, I plowed ahead. It turns out, the kid didn't quite understand the rules and next thing I know, his hand shoots up.

I was pretty new to being on the back side of a pulpit, but from what I remember growing up in church, I couldn't think of a single time I'd ever seen this happen. I'd never even heard of it happening, and I wasn't sure what the proper etiquette was in this situation. I kind of assumed a mother, or well-meaning nearby parent, would put a stop to his questioning, but his hand stayed up.

My best attempts to ignore him failed. To be honest, I liked his style, but even more than that, I just had to know what his question was, so I stopped.

"What can I help you with?"

"I've got a question for you, Mr. Kelly."

"Yes sir, I'll answer anything I can."

"How many people have you healed, Mr. Kelly?"

You can imagine the audience's response. Smiles and good natured chuckles all around and I had a hard time not laughing myself, but the question was an important one.

"0," I answered.

The young man's shoulders sank and his forehead wrinkled. I could see I was confusing him, so I put his mind at rest.

"I didn't heal anyone. Jesus healed every single one of them."

This seemed to satisfy him, but I needed to make one more thing clear.

"But, I'm not special. You can pray for people to be healed too. It doesn't take anything special, other than loving Jesus. Never forget that you can serve God just as good as I do."

That was it. Our total interaction was limited to his heckling and my response. I didn't get a chance to talk to him after the service. I hoped what I'd said had made an impact. From my perspective, I'd been open to the interruption and still managed to complete what God had sent me to do, but the incident was far from over.
What God was doing went well beyond me.

I think what happens is this -- I get it set in my head that the last thing God asked me to do is somehow my agenda. I tend to forget who's in charge. It's easy to think I chose my own path. That I picked the next target to love on, but if I stop for even an instant and think back I realize it's not true.

In every action I've taken, it was His hand leading me, and when it's not, I feel it.
But what if these things weren't interruptions? What if something else was going on? What if we're working on accepting interruptions, when all the time, we weren't being interrupted at all, just moving on to what's next?

This is a change in perspective. When you start to think of the interruptions as part of the plan, something cool happens. You begin to expect it.

Remember what we said about expectations? They open us up to possibilities we might not otherwise have seen, and they engage our faith, so that what we expect, becomes inevitable to us.

How finely tuned was Phillip's hearing that he picked up, not just that God was asking him to go, but that he knew exactly when and where? Unless he had become accustomed to the interruptions, it seems unlikely that it would have played out like it did.

Let's be honest. Most of us probably would have kept on preaching, at least gotten through that sermon. We would have finished the chicken dinner and then maybe we would check into transportation to this desert road.

By the time we decide to obey, I wonder how many times we miss our appointment with the Eunuch? Think about it. If our buddy Phil had just delayed a few hours, the chariot would have passed the point where they met, and the Eunuch might never have had the scripture explained, Ethiopia might have waited centuries to hear the Gospel.

How many times in my life, have I done what He asked, just a moment too late, then assumed I didn't hear at all, when my divine appointment didn't materialize?

That's why it's essential that we be open to God's agenda, because that's what it is. These weren't interruptions in the life of Phillip or His son. They were a part of the plan all along. The amazing discovery that I've made is that God's agenda is hidden in what often feels like an interruption.

Phillip couldn't see history from beginning to end. All he could see was Samaria, and they needed him badly.

But God could. God looked down through space and time and saw the impact that Eunuch would have, long before he was ever born, or put into service.

It must have seemed like an interruption to this young man, to become a eunuch at all. Talk about a mixed blessing. You can be put in charge of the Queen's court, but, you have to give up your ability to reproduce.

But, had he not been a eunuch, he likely would never have been trusted to carry out the tasks he was given. Those tasks were what allowed him the freedom to travel to Jerusalem to worship. God's agenda in this man's life may seem unusual, but it was His plan to plant the seeds of the Gospel in an entire continent.

Church has many agendas. We have them for our worship services, our building projects, our missions funds. We write agendas for nearly everything we do. While I do think God expects and honors us putting things in order, I wonder how much we miss when we stubbornly follow "God's plan" and ignore the detours.

That's why, when we started the Reckless Love Revolution, we added being open to interruption as one of our primary principles. Over time, I've come to see that this is the best way to stay on track with God's agenda for the ministry.

In my humanity, I think I see what He's about. In His divinity, He only shares enough with me to keep me from jacking things up too bad.

I'm not sure of all the reasons He only gives us one step at a time. Part of it is wrapped up in how we complicate things. If God showed us His whole plan, as likely as not, we'd immediately begin to streamline and "improve" on it.

For example, if He'd said to me, "Go preach and this kid is going to interrupt you and ask you how many people you've healed."

I know me. I would have stayed up the night before coming up with a good answer, which I would have been too tired to remember the next morning.

But, because, in my mind, the sermon was God's agenda, I kept my answer short, sweet and to the point.

A while later, a story was submitted to our website. The youth from the church I'd been preaching at had decided to put into practice what they'd heard in my message. So, with a stack of Why cards in hand, they headed out to a local park to minister.

While they were there, several of the kids spotted an older woman who was struggling to walk and seemed to be in a lot of pain. They asked if they could pray for her. It's stories that like this that keep us going.

From the inspiration of an interrupted sermon, this youth group had launched their own Reckless Love campaign and it sounded like they were doing it right. It made me feel good to know that the young man's question hadn't derailed God's intent for that church. But, I still didn't quite get the point.

Along with their story, the group had sent some photos and I remember looking down through them, then pausing on one. There was the woman the story had described, surrounded by several of the kids from their youth group. What I saw next, raised the hair on the back of my neck. Right in the center of the group was a familiar looking young man. I clicked on the photo to enlarge it, and suddenly, everything became clear. The last time I'd seen the boy in the center of the photo, he'd been raising his hand to ask me a question in the middle of my sermon. A faux pas of biblical proportions. The same hand that rested on the woman in the photo as this young man asked God to heal her broken body.

We experience moments in life that in one fraction of a second, shed light back along the path illuminating events much farther back than the time it takes to understand. In that instant, God showed me that what I'd thought of as an amusing detour in the middle of my carefully prepared sermon, was the entire reason for the journey in the first place.

Now, I see a chain of events that felt like annoying inconveniences that were the main course. I thought I was there to preach to a congregation of adults, but in fact, I was there to ordain and release a young minister of the Gospel to engage in Reckless Love.

God couldn't share all of this with me from the beginning. He needed me to experience one step at a time.

In my mind, there was a better way to train this young man to minister. But, if I'd done that, would he have had the courage to not just join in, but lead that group in prayer?

I doubt it.

But as soon as he heard me tell him he could do it, his faith was engaged. In that moment, this kid, who'd skirted the rules to get his answer, began expecting things from God. Not only that, but he was ready to pay the price, even if that meant asking a total stranger permission to pray for them in a public park.

God's agenda was so much better than my sermon, it put it to shame.

It's easy for those of us who've walked with God for a long time to make assumptions. We take for granted that we understand something about the way ahead. We think we know how to minister, what to say and do to open hearts and minds to the Gospel, but so many times, God's agenda isn't ours. His is written between the lines. He works, around, above and below us, as much as He works through us.

There are times I feel like I get more right by accident than on purpose.

Don't take this to mean you shouldn't set an agenda. After all, God's people perish for lack of vision. Laying a plan is the best way to get people committed to stepping out and getting them involved. When they know what's expected of them, it's easier for them to commit.

But, we can't become so in awe of our own great planning skills that we don't leave room for the Spirit.

That incident reminds me of a story from the ministry of Jesus.

People began bringing their children to Him to lay His hands on them. It says even nursing infants, and much like sticking your hand up in the middle of a sermon, this went against unspoken rules and traditions.

Children were never engaged publicly in the things of God in a meaningful way and the well-meaning disciples took offense. They started telling these parents to keep their kids under control in no uncertain terms, but Jesus stepped in.

"Whoa, hold up. I want these kids to come up here. Bring them up here, look guys, let them come. Don't you get it? Everyone in my kingdom is like a little kid. If you can't understand that, I'm sorry, but you'll never get in. You need to accept what I'm saying with childlike faith in order to understand it."

Now that I've got kids, I can tell you, their lives are all one big interruption. They play with this, and immediately drop it for that if it's shinier. They'll abandon something they just screamed to get in curiosity over a sudden noise. They are always up for new things, and up to a certain age, they'll try almost anything you give them.

I think this sense of wonder and excitement is something we're lacking in our approach to ministry too.

We want to be like the disciples, "Hey, it's time to pay attention to this, not that."

We want to control and guide people into an experience with God. We often insist that conditions surrounding our presentation of the Gospel have to be a certain way, but God will use whatever He needs to get our attention.

Even if it's inspiring a little boy to interrupt the guest speaker with a silly question.

I'm sure he wasn't the only one in that sanctuary that needed to hear that answer.

God uses the foolish things of the world to confound the wise, and often, while we're busy presenting a sound theological argument for faith, He's sneaking in under people's guard, between the lines. The Gospel is about being free from whatever holds you captive that isn't Him.

When we go out to share it with people, we need to be mindful of that.

One final word on God's interruptions. We tend to think that "orthodoxy" is the final word. There are things we do, and things we don't do in sharing the Gospel, but I want to say be careful. Sometimes we get into the habit of thinking that the way we do thing is the way it's always been done or the only way.

If I've learned anything in my study of Scripture, it's that God is full of surprises, and He's in the business to relating to us. Whatever He needs to do to make that happen. Don't discount something just because it doesn't fit your preferred method. Whatever you hear God say, do it now. You'll never be disappointed.

Don't get in the habit of thinking of the Bible as a list of don'ts. It's so much more than a book of rules.

It's a love story between a Creator so passionate, that when the world He built fell, He sacrificed Himself to restore that relationship. It's a love story about you, and He'll do anything that doesn't violate His nature to get to you, and that's exactly how He feels about those we are trying to reach. It's about love.

CHAPTER 11
"Is This Love That I've Been Searching For"
- Whitesnake

Just like it doesn't always make sense to love the people God calls us to minister to, His calling doesn't generally fit our profile either. People are always asking us about our story wherever we go, and I always defer to Ryan, because while I grew up in a Protestant, charismatic family, Ryan's family was super Mormon, or that's the way I see it.

He was even a distant relative to the prophet of the Mormon church, Gordon B. Hinckley. Talk about a lot to live up to. The way God caught Ryan's attention is pretty epic, but I should let him tell it, since I know I'm going to screw it up.

> As a kid in Idaho, there was nothing more normal than growing up Mormon. There were a couple of things that set me apart, however. First off, Gordon B. Hinckley, the prophet of the Mormon church at the time, sharing my last name brought some unwanted attention to bear on me. Also, my parents were divorced, which is unusual, but not unheard of. Because of that, I grew up in two households. My mom and her husband had two other sons and one daughter, while my dad and his wife had two daughters and one son.

I experienced the usual struggles with living in a broken home, but other than that, things probably weren't that different from many of your childhoods. We went to church on Sundays. It was very traditional and included a lot of rituals, which, as a youth, I grew really bored with. In fact, I can't remember ever experiencing the presence of God in a meaningful way, except during Christmas, when our focus shifted to songs about Jesus. This early experience with God's spirit would be key in leading me to become a follower of Jesus, which at the time, I thought I was.

Outside of church, nothing existed in my world that didn't revolve around basketball. From the moment I first set foot on a court, all I dreamed about was playing or working out to get better at playing. With each level I advanced, the goal became to play at the next level. I wanted to play college basketball more than anything, and as that day approached, it looked like I had a good chance. This created a drive in me to give 100% to achieve that dream.

There was only one thing standing in my way: my Mormon mission.

For those who don't know, as a young Mormon male, it is expected you will dedicate two full years of your life at 19 years old, to help spread the Mormon gospel.

At the time, the pressure I felt from my family, and my then-girlfriend, who insisted she would never marry anyone who wasn't a returned missionary.

The pressure felt unrelenting. In my mind, it was the only way to make my parents happy, keep my girlfriend happy, and for me, I needed to know if this God thing was real, or what? So, I decided to put a pin in my basketball career and accept my mission. It's a big deal in a young Mormon's life to get the "call to mission, " and when mine came, I was excited.

I was being sent to Scotland, which sounded great! It would give me a chance to get outside my sheltered existence. Just God and me. My prayer was just simply, "God I want to really know you."

As a follower of the Mormon tradition, I'd grown up on stories of the founder Joseph Smith and what he claimed was a vision from God to found the Mormon church. I was excited, because I believed my experience would be similar and I couldn't wait for God to be real to me.

Before being sent to Scotland, I was sent, along with other potential missionaries to Provo, Utah for my final training. There I spent three weeks, shedding my outside distractions, reading the Book of Mormon, and studying the lessons we would use in our evangelism.

It was like being in a spiritual prison, as all contact from the outside world was cut off, and your time was dedicated to forced readings from the book of Mormon. I was very curious why they put so much focus on that but only chose a few verses from the Bible to memorize. My prayer to know God lay wrapped inside that puzzle, as I would later discover.

I arrived in Scotland, and thought nothing of turning over my passport to our mission president on the first day, for "safe keeping." At the time, I couldn't see that this would be a challenge later, when I wanted to leave.

They kept us pretty busy and the first few months flew by. I missed family and friends, but I wanted to get closer to God, and following instructions was what I had been taught was the path to that. So, every day, I accepted my assignments, going door to door, to teach the Scottish people about Joseph

Smith and Jesus, through the material we'd been trained to share.

It didn't take long for me to miss being on the court. After all, I'd played nearly every day of my life before leaving for Provo. So, when I saw a poster one day for basketball tryouts, I was intrigued. Now, roommates on mission, are more like minders. They go everywhere with you, to keep you on track, and you keep track of them.

So, I asked my roommate, "Hey, think it would be okay for me to go to this tryout. I know I don't have time to play on the team, but just getting my hands on a ball would feel really good right now."

He agreed and went along with my lie that we were staying in for the evening and off we went.

From the smell of the court to the touch of the ball, everything about that night was almost magical. The release I felt from the weight of my daily schedule was amazing. It felt really good to be playing again, and I felt like I did really well. Which is why I was a little sad to leave, knowing there was no way I'd make it on the team, or be able to compete even if I did.

Two nights later, the phone rang.

"Hi, is this Ryan?"

"Yeah, who is this?"

"This is the coach of the basketball team you tried out for, calling to tell you, you're on the roster."

My heart jumped into my throat. Here was a golden opportunity, but I knew I couldn't accept it. I had to tell him the truth. "Well, I'm sorry, sir. I can't accept, I'm on a Mormon mission for two years, and I came to the tryout just to get on a court for a few hours."

"Well, we'd really like to see you play, so, let me know what we can do to make this work," the coach said.

"I'm sorry, there's just no way. I've got mission work all day, until into the evening. I'd love to play, but I can't make your practice schedule."

"Look, Ryan, I'm going, to be honest with you, you're one of the best players who came to try out. Why don't we do this, I'll move the practices to evenings. We'll meet at 9 PM to work around your schedule. Can you make that work?"

My heart was thumping so hard. I wanted this so bad. Basketball was my dream, and here was God, dropping a chance to play internationally right in my lap. Even though I knew it went against pretty much every rule of the mission, surely God wouldn't want me to turn this down. Besides, it was just a harmless game, and I'd still do what they asked of me during the daytime.

So, I roped my roommate into my little scheme, and he agreed to cover for me when necessary. It was going to be tricky.
While the practices were moved to the evenings, once competition started, the games were during the day.

So now, in addition to lying to pretty much everyone in my life, I had to work around the team schedule and still try to meet my obligations to my mission. All the while praying, "God, I want to know you."

Then came the day when a tournament in Aberdeen Scotland brought about a huge good news/bad news scenario that would change everything.

On the good side, I was playing great, averaging over 20 points a game and loving every second.

The bad news was, I was caught.

The next day my mission president called me to ask how things were going.

"It's going really well. I'm enjoying my mission and..."

"Well, Ryan here's the thing. You made the paper."

"Sweet, er, I mean, oh, that..."

"Meet me in my office tomorrow. We need to discuss what we're going to do about this situation."

That night I went to bed, incredibly nervous about what I would say in the meeting the next morning. But I really shouldn't have worried. The meeting never came. Sometime in the middle of the night, four other Mormon missionaries showed up at our flat.

Two of them began packing my things, while the other two berated me for abandoning my mission.

I was scared. For good reason as it turned out.

For the next little while, my life started to feel like something I'd seen in a movie. I was hustled out of my flat, and the five of us and my stuff took a little train ride.

They wouldn't say where we were going. I was mad. I felt betrayed and frustrated. I'd lost track of my desire to know God and was focused on my rage over being kidnapped.

They took me to the northern end of Scotland where I wasn't even allowed to contact my coach to let him know what had happened. I couldn't even call home.

Instead, I had a nice chat with my mission president, who informed me under no uncertain terms that things would be different from here on out. "I'd be very careful about your next move, Ryan. From now on, I've got eyes on you at all times."

I felt horrible. Not only had I been ripped away from something that I felt really good about, but I felt as if I'd abandoned my team.

So, I started looking for stray coins on the ground and secretly saving them up to make a phone call. Finally, I had enough.

"Coach? It's me, Ryan. I can't really explain everything, but I wanted you to know I'm okay."

"Where are you? I'll come get you. It's not right you're being treated this way."

"I appreciate that, but I think I need to finish this, good luck."

When I hung up, I felt like I was hanging up on life. It was the end of my international basketball career, and any hope, in my mind, of me being happy anytime soon. I could feel bitterness rising in me, and it was aimed at God for letting this happen.

As I trudged through my mission work half-heartedly, an escape plan began to form in my mind. I'd saved up enough to call my coach, so I continued my coin hunting, with the goal of calling my mom. Here I was, a grown man who'd given up his passport, feeling trapped in a foreign country, the whole thing seemed so ludicrous.

At that point, the idea of me serving God full-time was the last thing on my mind. I felt like if I could just reach my mom, she'd get me out of this mess. It was the only thing keeping me going.

When I finally had enough to make the international call, I felt so relieved. I'd switched from praying, "God, I want to know you," to "God, do whatever you have to, to get me out of here." And now it was finally going to be over.

After countless times of pretending to tie my laces as I scooped up stray coins, my bitterness was about to turn to rage. Instead of the compassion I'd imagined, my mother was furious. She told me in no uncertain terms that I would finish my mission. There was no way I was coming home early to embarrass the family and smear the Hinckley name. I know she meant well, but that didn't help.

I was trapped at the top of Scotland, alone, and no one even cared.

For months, I pleaded with God to get me home, and every time I talked to my mission president, I begged to be sent back to the states. If I could just get back to the US, I could make my way home. After nine months of what felt like hell in Scotland, I finally got some good news. My mission president called.

"Ryan, there's been an emergency transfer to North Carolina, do you want it?"

Did I want it? Of course, I wanted it. It was the first time I'd felt real joy since that night the four "missionaries" had come into my apartment and dragged me off to the ends of the earth.

But even then, as angry and frustrated I was with God, with my family, with the mission president, God had me right where he wanted me.

On my arrival in North Carolina, I was greeted by the mission president who was very nice. It was a bright spot in a dark experience. So, I stayed for a couple of months, but never forgot about my plan to hitch a ride back to Utah, or Idaho, where I knew people who could help me. Finally, I found someone.

I packed a bag, but the night before I was set to leave, once again, my mission president found out. This time, however, things were different.

Instead of being Shanghaied to North Dakota, or some Florida backwater, I was handed a ticket home.

I was greeted with disappointment. My family was frustrated and sad that I hadn't been able to complete my mission. Right here, though, I have to say I was relieved at this reaction, for one reason. Other people I knew of had come home early, to find the door locked and their family refusing to acknowledge their existence. It could have been much worse.

But, that didn't stop me from feeling mad at God. After all, he'd allowed me to go through all of this pain. Had it not been for basketball, my downward spiral would have taken place a lot faster. I was given a scholarship to play basketball at Treasure Valley Community College, where I started for two years.

My focus on basketball kept me out of trouble. I loved playing, and I'd experienced losing this once already and didn't want to ruin it. It kept me close to home, which allowed me to build better relationships with my mom and dad.

God, on the other hand, was still an open question for me. I knew He was there, but I didn't want anymore to do with Him than I had to. From there, I went on to a year on the Nebraska Cornhusker's team. After that, I transferred to Bellevue University in Omaha, Nebraska.

Without any real foundation in Jesus, ironically, the namesake of the church I'd grown up in, my life with God was shaky at best, and soon, I walked away from Him entirely.

After college, I took a job as a trade show pitchman, selling products at fairs and conventions. I traveled from one car show and home show to another, town to town across the map. It was a hard life. I enjoyed the travel, and I started to feel like a rockstar and what does a rockstar do, but party?

The drugs and alcohol seemed like such a release after my buttoned-down upbringing, and it was fun, for a while. But what I couldn't see was what it was doing to my life.

I managed to keep pace for several years until even some of the hard core partiers started worrying that I might not live too much longer. I can remember the moment when I finally heard them and thought, "They're right, Ryan, if you don't change, something bad's going to happen."

But I felt powerless to stop myself.

Then, it came to a crashing halt in October of 2001.

I was on the top floor of one of the best hotels in Las Vegas. We'd rented the whole thing, and I was there to party for a solid week. To kick things off, I took seven hits of a drug called Ecstasy, preparing to hit the town with my friends. But, instead of the glorious high I was expecting, a serious feeling of conviction came over me.

From somewhere deep in my memory, the prayer that had launched me into my mission came back, "God I want to know you."

I remember looking at myself in the mirror, crying out to God that if He was there, I was ready!

I instantly came back to my right mind. It seemed like a miracle.

Instead of going out, I stayed in and made arrangements to change my flight to the next day, arriving in Oakland, California for my next show several days ahead of schedule, which turned out to be perfect timing.

On my arrival in Pleasanton, California, there was a gift waiting for me. I met a beautiful girl, Cynthia, who would later become my wife and life partner. If I was writing this story, it would end here, happily ever after, but that's not exactly what went down.

At that point, I knew God existed. He'd interrupted my high and introduced me to the love of my life, but I had no idea what to do next. Cynthia and I struggled to understand who Jesus was to us and what our life would look like going forward. We knew we were in love and decided to get married, but found that without God at the center of our relationship, making it work was hard.

Six months later, she became pregnant with our first son, Aiden.

Becoming a father was a sobering turning point for me. I knew it was time to change.

I gave up smoking and drugs and got control over my alcohol consumption, something I'd grown up believing was completely wrong. I still wasn't sold out on the God thing, but I knew I didn't want to be a hypocrite when it came time to teach my children how to make these choices in their own lives.

But, through it all, God had his hand on me. After getting married, life on the road was out.

I took a job with Footlocker. My background in athletics made this a "shoe in," and I became a manager trainer.

They moved us around a lot, starting in Las Vegas, then Missoula, Montana before we transferred to Tulsa, Oklahoma. With each step in our journey, we grew a little closer to God. Our relationship became stronger, and church became something we both enjoyed.

Although we had settled into a congregation, through some friends who had moved to a new church, we decided to try it, and it was at Destiny Life that I finally found what I'd been looking for.

While I'd been excited about church, I was still compartmentalizing. I had my church life, and my day-to-day life, and while my faith definitely shaped my actions, they weren't fully merged.

Shortly after our transition there, I had an experience that I will never forget.
At 3 AM I woke up, whether from an audible voice, or part of a dream I don't know. But, I heard a voice saying, "Wake up."

It was so clear, it scared me. I grabbed a bat, sure someone was in the house. After checking every room, my pulse finally settled, and I went back to sleep.

Soon, I heard the voice again. "Wake up!"

Again, I checked the house carefully. This time I was too shaken up to go back to bed, so I turned on a podcast from Carl Lentz, "That girl is poison," which I chose because the title sounded cool.

Deep, huh?

It wouldn't have mattered which title I chose, though, because as soon as it started, I began to weep as God radically grabbed my heart.

Now, I have to tell you, I've never been much of a reader. I bet I could count the books I had read, that weren't required, on one hand up until that point. But that night, something changed. I woke the next morning with insatiable desire to read the Bible and anything I could find about God.

I consumed over 50 volumes in the next year.

I read through the New Testament in two weeks flat.

I couldn't get enough.

Then I started having visions. In my dreams, God was calling me to preach! So, I reasoned, "Preachers write sermons."

I'd never done it, but if that's what I was going to be, why not?

I started writing. I'd never been asked to speak before, but as soon as the sermon was finished, my church asked me to preach! Although I'd said nothing about writing a sermon, my pastor just sensed that I had something to say.

Almost overnight, our marriage went from a frustrating struggle to a peaceful place we wanted to spend time in! God was changing everything.

Over the next couple of years, opportunities to preach would just come up. The Spirit was teaching me things, and as fast as I learned them, I would share them. Not only that, but relationships started to materialize around me with people God wanted in my life. Then it happened.

Judah Smith came to town. I loved his preaching, and I knew that if I wanted a good seat, I had to get there early. So, I showed up three hours beforehand. And there, on the sidewalk, was a man I've now grown to think of as my brother.

There, in front of Guts church, we became friends.

Suffice it to say, out of this seemingly "chance meeting" a beautiful friendship, the Reckless Love Revolution and the book you're reading was born.

And there you have it, folks. Straight from Ryan's mouth, what a story!

I don't really have a lot to add, except this, even if you grow up in a place that is confused about the identity of Jesus, run away from him into sports, drugs and a self-centered life, don't think that's going to excuse you from the call of God on your life. Just as we are called to love those that it doesn't make sense, His call rarely makes sense by our standards either.

CHAPTER 12
"What The World Needs Now, Is Love, Sweet Love"
- Jackie DeShannon

We've defined what Reckless Love looks like, we've talked about the logistics of it, but now it's time to get real. Right now, where you are, I want you to think about something. What are you going to do about it?

Up until now, it's all just words on a page. As the old saying goes, it's all fun and games until...well, until is right now.

You're running out of book and at the end of this whole thing I'm going to challenge you to put your beliefs into action, so what's that going to look like for you? What will you do? Where will you start? Who will work with you? What if no one does?

So, let me just answer this right here.

You.

You were called to love your neighbor as yourself. You weren't called to make anyone else do it. Not that you shouldn't encourage them to. But if you find yourself as the only one, just start. Trust me on this.

When I first got the message about teaching the world to love in a whole new way, I thought I was alone in it, but the fire was burning so hot in my spirit that I knew it didn't matter.

If, and I say if because you're rarely alone, but if you find yourself the only one in your congregation willing to step out, fine. Don't sweat it. Here's the thing. Like I've said, this love stuff is contagious, and it may just be that you need to reach out right inside your own congregation.

See, the power of love is not just for salvation. Sure, the outside world needs it, but it doesn't stop there. We're going to talk more about the " bus stop" mentality here in a bit, but suffice it to say that just because you're inside the four walls, so to speak, doesn't mean your ministry to love ends.

No. Sometimes it's needed even more inside the church. Christians can be cruel.

Jesus told a story about a king who had a servant. The servant owed the king a lot of money. The king brought the servant in and said he was going to throw him and his family into prison if the man could not pay. But, the servant threw himself on the king's mercy, he begged for forgiveness, and he got it. Later, the king heard from others of this man's treatment of one of his fellow servants. It seems this other servant owed the forgiven man a small debt of a few dollars.

But, rather than extend the mercy he'd been given, he treated the man horribly and threw him in prison.

Too many times, we act like that forgiven servant. We forget we have no place in God's kingdom without the love He first showed us. So, we tend to be unforgiving and even judgmental at times.

Showing weakness inside the church can be dangerous. Our fellow believers, who should show us grace, are often unmerciful and cruel.

Love is always welcome. So, start there. Reckless Love is always unexpected because it makes no sense.

Jesus taught us to love our enemies. He seemed to think it was no great feat to love those who loved us first.

The king, after seeing that his gift of grace had meant nothing, took it back. He threw the man into prison until he paid his debt. Don't be like that servant.

Love will cost you. It's not free. It's not even cheap. But compared to the cost of unforgiveness and a lack of compassion for your fellow man, it's a good investment. The Church needs to be reminded of what love looks and feels like, and that might just start with you.

Once you've opened the box, so to speak, you won't be able to contain it. Trust me. Once you've engaged in Reckless Love just one time, you'll be begging God to show you who's next. You'll be looking for targets to the point it almost becomes an addiction. It feels good to extend the hands of Jesus for no reason other than because He first loved you.

But, it won't stop there. The givers of Reckless Love aren't the only ones changed by it. Those they love are impacted for life.

When you open up your heart, even inside your church community, it will begin a revolution. You can't stop it. Once they've seen the results, you'll have no problem convincing them to engage, and those that won't will be left behind.

It's okay. Not everyone gets it.

Jesus said it a lot. He said things like, "If you set up to start plowing in the kingdom, then start, only to change your mind and walk away, don't bother coming back, you're not the right kind of person to help build the kingdom."
In fact, if you find yourself inside a faith community that can't see the vision for the Reckless Love Revolution because they're too busy with their agendas, that's the perfect place to start. They need it.

How can we ever hope to switch our mentality from running inside the walls to hunker down and wait for a way out, to restore God's creation to Him, if we don't understand love ourselves?

Some of you are saying, "Well, I'm not ordained, or the leadership of my church would never let me minister."

I'm here to tell you, the same as I said to the young man who interrupted my sermon, "Yes, you are."

You are just as called and ordained as anyone, and anyone who says otherwise doesn't understand this love we're talking about.

If you exist inside a congregation that is so controlled you cannot extend Reckless Love without fearing reprisals, get out. I hate to tell you, but that has nothing to do with Jesus or his church.

Sometimes what looks like kingdom to us, has more in common with Babel.

The tower of Babel was a technological marvel of its time. It was a tower designed to reach up to heaven. Some say they intended to go up and ask God to answer them, become His equal in some way. Whatever the purpose, it caught His attention. In fact, it troubled God to the point that He decided He had to do something to stop them. He saw that they were all of one mind and He knew whatever they decided to do, they could achieve it. Without God, that would never end well.

So, God determined to put a stop to it by confusing their language. When the men returned to work the next day, they found that none of them could converse with each other. Where there had been a powerful sense of unity before, without communication, cooperation broke down. They couldn't explain what needed to be done. So, one by one, they walked away. Without the ability to speak a common language, they couldn't complete the work.

Too many times, what we've built on the "rock" Jesus laid, looks more like this tower than His church. But, if the pagan masses of the ancient world could achieve something as great as this with their unity, think what the church of Jesus Christ could do if we were all in agreement.

What is this message that could bring us all together, across the denominational lines, across doctrinal lines that have no bearing on eternity? I think it's love.

This is what you're being called to. This is what I'm challenging you to be a part of. I don't see this as a local "revival" or even a renewal movement limited to just one country, or even one continent. I think this is the spark that could light a revival that would sweep the world. We've already seen the power of love in our society, through the Jesus movement of the 1960s and 70s, what if it had been coupled with the true understanding that we love, not just for the sake of love, but because of the love He showed for us.

What if what the world needs now is truly love? But not of a temporary, romantic nature, or some sentimental ideology, but real love.

Love with power and grace and mercy at its core.

Unconditional, eternal love of a kind not truly experienced except through one man, Jesus.

What if we are the only ones that can bring it to them? What if you are the only one that can start it where you are? Are you ready?

We could achieve what no army, no king, no president, no revolution of men could ever make possible. We could change the world and bring it back to its Creator.

I'm convinced this is exactly what He had in mind from the very beginning. A revolution without a single shot fired that could carry every kingdom, every corporation, every nation and state before it.

How else could we ever find ourselves in the world that was spoken of by the prophets? Where men turned their swords into plows and stop practicing the art of war? I can't think of any other way, can you?

This is so much bigger than me, or you or all of the people we've ever known. It's going to take everything we can give it, and we're going to have to call for reinforcements to get the word out, but they'll come.

This is the Gospel that spread once before. Not a religion, or denomination, but a story about the love of a God that could not walk away from His creation.

But it all has to start with you.

That's why I wrote this book. I'm only one man, and Ryan and I can only travel to so many places. But this book can find you wherever you are and share this challenge. Will you accept it?

If so, we're going to get real in these last few chapters. We're going to talk about some hard truths. We're going to take a hard look at some things that need to change, and we're going to paint a picture of what this can look like if we truly carry it out.

I'm so freaking excited.

To know that I get to be a part of this great adventure with you, that is what keeps me awake at night. That's what I see when standing on a stage, or a football field. That's what I hear when I listen to youth singing praise. That's what gets me up in the morning and keeps me leaving my family to go and preach.

Without that vision of the world that could be something more, could be what we all hope for, it wouldn't be worth it. No other dream is big enough, as you'll see when I share my story.

So, as you read this last section, I want you to think about your part in it. I want you to open your eyes for opportunity and your ears for the father's voice. I want you to catch my excitement and be ready to move when He calls. I want to encourage you to be brave and courageous because He's going to challenge you. I want you to get up, and out of your comfort zone. It's pretty there, but remember, nothing grows in them. And as you do, please, share this book and this challenge wherever you go. You don't have to use my words, it's not about me, but put it out there.

As you begin to catch a vision, don't wait. If you finish this book before you engage in your first act of Reckless Love, I've failed. I hope that it's burning in you so strong by now that you haven't waited for my permission. But, if you have, don't any longer, it's time.

The world cannot wait for the love of Jesus. It needs it now and now and now and now. And in every moment, more lives are coming into existence that will need to hear about this wonderful God who loved us so much, He gave Himself in Reckless Love to start this revolution. Let's go!

CHAPTER 13
"When Love Calls, You'd Better Answer"
- Atlantic Starr

As Americans, we tend to see people's actions in a kind of hierarchy of honor. At the top of the stack, we place things we see as being sacrificial or giving. We use the title hero to refer to those who would risk their lives in service.

Sacrifices are important. God's entire relationship to man is based on them to one degree or another, but there's an interesting story that I think illustrates a good point.

Saul is king in Israel, and Samuel is serving as judge and prophet. Saul has led the army into battle against their enemies, and he received specific instructions to not leave any of them alive. But as he returns to meet with Samuel, he brings some flocks. Samuel hears them bleating, and he asks Saul what he's done.

Saul, being caught, tries to turn it into a good thing. It seems a shame to waste all of that good, sacrificial meat, he states. Surely God would want the best of their flocks for Himself.

Samuel says this phrase that sticks with me, "What do you think God wants more? Hmm? Your animal sacrifices, or for you, His servant to listen to His voice and obey Him? Pay attention! Obedience is much more important than any burnt offering and your submission to Him, your sacrifice of your own pride, is much more pleasing than a prize ram!"

Samuel was ticked off! It wasn't the first time Saul had acted on his own and disobeyed God. Samuel was tired of going through the motions of hearing from the Lord, bringing God's word to Saul, and being ignored.

You can imagine. It's like your boss hires you to do a job and advise him, then he throws out all your research and does it his own way, completely disregarding you. But, of course, your boss would be God in this analogy, so that's way worse, right?

Sometimes, in our human understanding, we think the "sexy" important stuff in life is what we should be focused on. We want to not only be useful; we want to be important. We want to feel good about what we do, and we want people to notice us, too.

So, it's easy sometimes, to assume that the little, detailed projects God sends us to do are not as important as the big glamorous ones.

See, Saul had issues. He wanted to be seen as important. He was constantly struggling with his place in the kingdom. It wasn't enough to be chosen by God. He wanted to win the "popular vote" too. So, he was fond of doing things to make that happen, like sparing a few princesses and some sheep.

He was a lot like us. Then, he'd complain when things weren't going well with his monarchy. Sound familiar?

The trouble with it was, God needed his obedience. Since the people had chosen to listen to a king, rather than God directly, through Samuel, he mattered. A lot.

See, the people's blessings lay on the other side of Saul's obedience. In fact, the entire kingdom suffered because of his disobedience.

I know, most of us aren't in positions of that much influence, so it's a little different, but the principle is the same. Someone else's blessing often lies on the other side of our obedience.

In fact, I'm almost inclined to think that the less we want to do a thing God tells us to do, the more likely it is that thing is for someone else's benefit more than ours. When it's for us, it's easy.

"Go apply for this big important job," we hear.

"Yes God, right away," we say.

It's easy to do things that benefit us directly. But, when the benefit is unclear, or maybe even completely hidden, it gets more challenging. But what if the thing God asks you to do is downright "wrong?"

By that, I don't mean morally wrong. God isn't like us; He doesn't tempt us to sin. But He can ask us to do things that make us feel awkward, afraid, or silly.

What then? The choice is always ours.

We've discussed this before, but God doesn't drag into obedience. That's because voluntary action is so much more powerful than anything you can be forced or coerced to do. When you choose it, you couple your will, with God's will and that, my friend, is some very powerful stuff.

He loves it. Especially when we do it out of obedience, rather than excitement over the expected outcome.

Ryan and I did not get into this for fame and glory. We're not out traveling the world for ourselves. We know that what we do doesn't always make sense to everyone. In fact, a lot of it looks downright foolish.

Sometimes, life with God is a puzzle. He tells us where to go, or what to do, but He leaves out a lot of the details.

We've got to work it out from the beginning to find out what it all means, and sometimes, we still don't understand it all, even when it's over.

Sometimes, we're a lot like an ant, walking across a big flat-screen TV. We can see a few pixels of what's going on in the movie below us, but we can't see the whole picture. Us, telling God that what He sends us to do, doesn't make sense. It's a lot like that ant telling you, "Your favorite show sucks," because of the six or eight pixels he can see at a time.

That's what really makes no sense.
 Sometimes it happens too fast to make sense of it. God speaks, and we have to choose, obey, or do our own thing. He doesn't stop loving us or using us either way. The choice is truly ours. But often we have to make it in just a few seconds.

I was in Dallas, Texas for a preaching gig. I was running a little late, as usual, and I needed some extra energy. Kick Start energy drinks are my poison of choice when I need it, and 7-Eleven is the best place to find a good selection. So I pulled off and stopped.
I staggered in and found the cooler. As I made my selection, for no particular reason, I found myself watching the cashier. It's a girl, and before I could even decide what I thought about her,

God told me to talk to her.

So, I turned back to the cooler, found my favorite flavor and made my selection. I took it up to the register and the whole way, I was kind of arguing back with God.

"I don't know what to say."

"Tell her I'm not angry with her."

"What?"

"You heard me. Tell me I'm not angry with her."
So, I put my drinks on the counter, and she started to ring me up.

"I don't even know if she knows You, or even believes in You," I tell God.

So, I decided a test was in order. If she knew God, I'd tell her.

I asked her a question that I figured was pretty safe and not too embarrassing.

"Are you having a good day? Is there anything I can pray for you about?"

I smiled, hoping I didn't look like a creeper, cause I sure don't look like a preacher.

She smiled at me, "Nope, everything is perfect."

I went back to arguing with God, "See, that's silly, she says everything is perfect."

"Tell her I'm not mad at her."

He's wasn't going to let up, and I knew I'd just be back if I left without doing it. So I took a deep breath and said, "God wants me to tell you He's not mad at you."

And I waited for a reaction.

Somehow, no matter how many times this sort of thing happens, I'm always surprised when people respond. I've had enough conversations with God to know when it's Him talking, but somehow, I always expect something different. I watched as the message settled in, and the girl stepped back and started to cry.

If you're a guy reading this, you know exactly how I felt. It's never good when a woman cries, ever. It's awkward, and we don't know what to do with it, and this was not much better.

"Are you okay?" I asked.

I'm not sure if I really wanted her to answer. I was short on time, and I'd just as soon get out of there before anyone else came in.

"No, I'm not, not really," she said.

"Last night, I came out to my parents. They didn't know I was a lesbian and it didn't go well."

She went on to explain that her parents had reacted badly and now she felt like there was no way for her to go on. She felt like the whole world was against her and she was pretty sure the God she'd grown up hearing about was extremely angry.

So, I asked God, "What do I say?"

But, here's the thing. It seems like a big deal before you step out and say what He tells you to, but once you do, the words have a way of showing up. In fact, the only time I ever feel that I don't know what to say is when it's best if I say nothing at all.

"God loves you. He always has. He has a plan for you, and this cannot separate you from Him," I said.
I asked the girl again if I could pray for her and she said yes.

So I did then I took my Kick Start, which I somehow didn't need so much at this point since moments like this are a big adrenaline rush. I went to preach my sermon.

It's kind of weird how it works sometimes. These little de-tours in my life sometimes feel like bombing runs into other people's lives because they are going through things I have no idea about. When God starts talking, it opens things up. People tell me things, they cry, they laugh, it's different every time, but it's always good.

So, remember King Saul. It didn't end so well with him. After he disobeyed God, Samuel continued. He reminded Saul that he had been anointed above all his brothers to rule over the tribes of Israel and that God himself had sent Saul against his enemies and He was not pleased with Saul's disregard for His orders. It had been a simple matter of following instructions, but Saul had clearly failed.

Rather than repent, even after Samuel has chastised him, Saul continued to operate out of his pride, something I do not recommend.

"I did what God said, I destroyed them all and brought back their king as prisoner. Some of the soldiers brought back sheep to worship your God. I don't see the problem."

This brings us back to where we came in. God desires obedience more than sacrifice. But Samuel wasn't finished with Saul, "I'm sorry to tell you that God's anointing does not come without some obligations. You've rejected Him, and now He has rejected you as king over Israel."

At this point, it would have been best for Saul, had he simply sought God's face for himself. But like so many, he didn't understand that this is what God had wanted all along. He believed that Samuel was the only way to get to God. Like a kid caught with his hand in the cookie jar, Saul folded. He cried, he begged forgiveness, he asked Samuel to come back with him, so that he could worship. He still didn't get it.

Fortunately for us, we live under a covenant of grace. God's mercy is new every morning, and Saul probably could have had it, had he been humble enough to let go of his own pride and beg forgiveness. With us, God isn't quick to give up, but we don't always get infinite chances every time.

Like I've said before, I've often wondered, who was the guy that passed up Reckless Love? Really, we'd like to know so we can send them a thank you card. I'm joking of course because they missed a great opportunity, but that could have been Ryan and me, had we not been ready to obey.

Obedience is a big deal, and you'll never know what it may mean to someone if you decide not to obey. Sure, we got to do Reckless Love, but what about the young people that first duo might have reached? Where are they now?

The children of Israel were in for a tough transition between Saul and David because of Saul's disobedience. I cannot be clear enough on this. It isn't just about you. You may be holding the key to someone's blessing.

When we obey, good things happen. Not only do we unlock things for others, but we unlock things in our own lives as well. When we obey, we make it possible for God to trust us with bigger things.

When we ignore what God has for us, we detour our progress, and often we have to start over. I don't mean to sound melodramatic, but how many times have you had to learn a lesson in life more than once, simply because you didn't do what you knew you needed to do the first time? I know for me, it's happened a lot.

God is so good to us though. He's always patient. If you ever feel that He is anything but love, you're missing it. That's not God. Not that He won't be disappointed, or disapproving, but in a kind, warm, loving, restoring kind of way. When you find yourself off track, He's the voice encouraging you to get back up and try again.

That other voice? That's the enemy, learn it well, and shut it out. Nothing it says bears listening to.

CHAPTER 14
"I Can't Do Anything Except Be In Love With You"
- Dire Straits

Probably the most shocking truth that God has hammered
home in my life throughout the formation of this ministry is
this: He uses the things that disqualify us in the world's eyes
to qualify us to what He's called us to.

The best example of this principle from the Bible happens
after the story I shared about King Saul. You remember how
he went to battle, with specific instructions, failed to fulfill
them, then rather than repent, just kept doubling down in his
pride, demanding Samuel, God's prophet, to help him out of
the jam he'd created for himself.

Finally, Samuel told him it was over. God had rejected him as
king.

What happens next sets up probably my greatest Biblical
hero, King David, to take the throne. Now that God had rejected Saul, Samuel had some work to do. As the prophet of
Israel, God tapped him to choose the next king. He told him
where to go to anoint the next king, and Samuel, whose
obedience was legendary, biblically speaking, grabbed his
cloak and his walking stick, a horn of anointing oil, and he
got out of town.

When he arrived at Jesse's house, he knew God had told him to come here to anoint the next king, but what happened next was a bit confusing. When Jesse brought out his sons to meet the prophet, something was off. Although Samuel assumed the oldest and best looking was the obvious choice, the next king was not there.

So, he asked Jesse, "What's up? I thought you brought all of your sons, but are you holding out on me?"

Jesse squirmed. Not because he didn't have another son, but because David, the youngest, the runt of the litter, was a bit of an embarrassment. He was brash and outspoken and not really someone they paraded in polite company. But since the prophet had asked, he sent to the fields for David.

Immediately, when Samuel saw him, he knew he was the one. It didn't matter that his dad had tried to hide him, or that his brothers made fun of even asking him to meet the prophet. They saw a skinny little kid, with a big mouth and a big heart, and a lot of crazy ideas, but God saw a man who would obey. God saw a friend and Israel's next king.

But, even after being anointed with oil by the prophet, it wasn't an easy road. David would wait years to even be considered for leadership at all, let alone the throne.

But he was king, and nothing else would satisfy the role he was supposed to play.

I know, because all of my life I knew I was supposed to be a preacher. I just knew. No matter how I tried to run away from it, or do other things in my own power, it didn't work out, but God had a plan.

See, God often tells us the future, long before we're ready to step into it. He told David he'd be king long before Saul left the throne. I felt called to preach long before I was ready. We both had things to learn. Mine included a lot of rough road and David had to fight a giant, among other things.

Picture this. The entire army is camped out, engaged in an epic battle against a rival nation. This nation, the Philistines, is famed for cruelty and things like human sacrifice. They're fierce warriors, and among their secret weapons is, this: genetically, they are predisposed to producing giants. For real. One giant, in particular, a clown named Goliath, was making a huge pain of himself.

Every single day, this guy would wade out into the battlefield and challenge the army of Israel. He'd fight their best guy. If he won, they'd be enslaved. If Israel's champion won, the Philistines would surrender and become their servants. But, no one would take his challenge.

It wasn't like they didn't have warriors. In fact, King Saul himself was a famed fighter. He had a body guard of elite soldiers, but this guy was over nine feet tall, with a spear the size of a beam. He had two guys carry his sword and shield to the battlefield each day.

The funny thing was, the Bible also tells us, that in his family, Goliath was the runt. His brothers were bigger. Maybe this accounts for his bad attitude.

I grew up a little like David. It's assumed he was about 13 when he met the giant in battle, and we'll get to that in a minute.

When I was thirteen, I was introduced to a giant of my own. I knew that I knew that I knew I was called to full-time, Christian ministry. I took the challenge seriously and began to serve with everything I had.

I worked in my church youth ministry. I engaged in Christian arts ministry. Heck, I even took ballet, as the only boy to serve God. I was serious.

The arts thing took off for me, and by the time I was eighteen, I was being offered a scholarship to study theater, and I knew this was what I wanted to do, serve God in the arts. But He had a different plan. I was packed and ready to head to school when He pulled me aside and told me to stay and intern under our then youth pastor.

I grew up in church, I had a great family, but I was ready to get out and stretch my wings. I wanted to do my own thing.

So, God had to interrupt me. It was one night during a revival that I heard God as clear as a bell tell me that college would have to wait, I needed to stay and intern.

At the same time, I was feeling the call to intern, God spoke to my youth pastor and told him to ask me to stay and intern for two years. So, I did.

But, on the side, the whole time, I had my own agenda. I wanted to be famous. I'd give God credit, once I got there, but make no mistake. People were going to know who Kelly Kopp was.

So, while I was interning, I started playing in a punk band. After my internship, I headed out on my own and got a gig as a youth pastor.
I was good at it. As I poured myself into the ministry, kids got involved.

The group, which started as seven kids, grew to seventy.
But, I felt like a fake.

Although I'd absorbed enough "church" to know the words to say, the right things to tell them to do, I didn't feel like I was living it. My life was not an example of what I knew was right, or what I wanted them to do.

One night, it all came to a head, "I'm not this guy. I'm not a youth pastor. I have a plan for my life, and this is not it," I said to myself.

So, after one evening service, I resigned. I was on my way, and I couldn't let a little thing like being called to ministry slow me down. All I wanted was to be famous.
For my whole life, I'd looked up to my dad, who is a great drummer. I'd learned to play bass and getting into bands was not a problem. I was a good musician. I showed up to practice, and I worked hard. I knew I could make it somehow. But one after the other, the groups would fall apart. It seemed very few wannabe rock musicians had my work ethic, go figure. Someone would get a job and leave without saying anything, or gear would get stolen, people would break up, or hook up, or get drunk and get friendly with the wrong guy or girl.

The drama was constant, the music suffered, and I was getting nowhere fast. I knew that if I was going to get what I wanted, I had to get out of that scene and work with some real pros.

I'd made some connections in the music industry, and I decided I needed to work in production. So, I started calling a guy in Midland, Texas who I knew was looking to hire. He said no.

For six months straight. He kept saying no, and I kept not giving up.

Finally, realizing my lease was up, and I had nowhere else to go, I made an offer he could not refuse.

"Okay I get you don't want to hire me, tell you what, why don't I prove my worth? I'll come down there and work for you for free. All I need is a place to crash and enough food to stay alive. You won't regret it."

While this particular chapter in my life is not one I want to be emulated, there is a valuable lesson right here. That if you want something bad enough, you will find a way to get it.

He finally said yes, and I sold my stuff, hitched a ride to Midland and moved in with one of his guys. That's how I started my music promotions career.

I was on my way to rock and roll stardom. I could feel it.

I know what you may be thinking, but this was the big leagues. The dude managed a few bands you might have heard of, like Nickelback and Cinderella. As far as a classroom for learning the tour management business, I could not have asked for a better laboratory.

For three months, I showed up every day, did whatever was asked of me and more. And never received a dime. Then came my big chance.

People in the music industry are notoriously emotionally driven, so it came as no big surprise when the boss' assistant quit on a moment's notice.

"Kelly, you've been hustling, and I'm giving you a big chance here, don't screw this up."

He named me his new assistant. It didn't take long at all from there before I was a paid professional tour manager. I was finally living the life I'd dreamed of when I'd hitched a ride here.

Within six months, I was on the road, managing my own tours, working with bad like, RED, 3 Days Grace, and Breaking Benjamin. I worked on the Warp Tour, and I thought, "Man, this is it!"

I had arrived. I wasn't famous yet, but I could see it from here. Getting further in would not be a problem.

I felt fulfilled. I was touring the country with some of the greatest music acts in the country, road tripping through my days and partying through my nights. I had arrived.

That's when it all came to a crashing halt, literally. I was on tour with RED. We'd been renting a bus and finally had made enough to buy our own tour bus. So, we trailered up the gear and rented a 15 passenger van to make the drive from South Carolina to Nashville to pick up our bus.

I was so stoked.

I'd been running so hard that I was exhausted. I crawled into one of the back seats and slept so hard I was practically in a coma, when just a few miles short of our destination, a highway worker's carelessness, changed my life.

Coming into Nashville in 6 AM rush hour traffic on unfamiliar roads, when our driver spotted a barrier rail, sticking out into the highway. There was no room to stop and no time to change lanes. With a rip, the sharp end of what should have been a safety barrier cut through our rented fifteen passenger van like a can opener ripping through a can of tuna.

As the van careened to a stop, I woke up, skipping down the highway on my back, having slid out of the van and onto the asphalt. I would later find out that 90% of the flesh on my back had been shredded, sending my body into shock. As I stopped, I looked up, seeing the members of the band in the van, my first thought was that, as their manager, I needed to check on them.

What I didn't know was that they were watching a truck bearing down on me, which would have crushed me, had it not been for the gear trailer protecting me. Later, I was told that had I not been sleeping at the time, so that my body was limp, the metal guard rail, which skimmed me, would have likely sliced my neck, leaving me to bleed out on the highway.

My injuries were severe enough that I required specialized treatment. So, for the next period of my life, I underwent treatment in a burn unit.

Out of some of the worst things come some of the best. During this time, I also started dating my now wife, Lindsay. However, even a series of near death experiences crammed into a single accident were not enough to get my attention. I still believed I was destined to be famous and the road beckoned.

I had a tough choice to make, and it's likely that love saved my life right here. I had to choose. Stay with Lindsay, or go back on the road, and likely out of her life for good.

I stayed.

For a long time, I was scared almost every time I drove. Any incident on the roadway would have me freaked out. I was terrified to sleep in a vehicle for a long time. The scars from something like that are deeper than just the physical.

Fame is a fickle mistress, and the music business was done with me if I couldn't get back on a tour bus. So, I needed a job. But, I wasn't done with Fame yet, whatever she thought of me. I was in it to win it.

I found a local TV station that needed an ad salesman, selling to businesses in West Texas and New Mexico, but I had a plan.

I could see that their lineup of local broadcasting and reruns lacked color and I knew just what it needed.

So, a month later, I pitched them my idea. A show, starring me and whatever others I could convince to join me. It would be a mix between "Wayne's World" (ask your dad, if you don't know) and "Jacka**." So, it was a family show...right....

Finally, my face was known in a two-state area, and I figured I could leverage that into a slot on a cable network, and from there, the world would be my oyster. But the world already had one: Johnny Knoxville and I guess they weren't ready for another.

So after 30 episodes, of what I thought was a smashing success, I was the first one on the chopping block when a new general manager came to town.

He couldn't stand my show, and there was no conversation to be had. I was fired within two weeks of his arrival. My dreams of fame and fortune had collapsed again, but still, I persisted. I took my ad sales experience and went to work for a newspaper, where I launched a magazine, along the same lines as my TV show, called The Pulse.

It just wasn't the same. The audience was too distant, and print media was in a steady decline.

So, I did what any artist in need of a steady gig would do. I went into the most notoriously cutthroat and unstable business of them all, comedy.

It was an easy in. I started by pitching event nights to clubs, an eco-system my touring days had made me intimately acquainted with. Their audiences were looking for entertainment, and I could provide it cheap.

I started out sponsoring game nights, trivia, and Let's Make a Deal. I could bring a bar up to capacity and have a line out the door in just a few nights of performing. They loved me, and I loved my job.

Eventually, I edited my show down to the thing I did best -- audience banter, and became a professional insult comic. Every night I was on, the owners could count on a full bar, and people came from all over to hear me spew horrible things at them. I was funny, no doubt, but words do hurt, and it came back on me.

I had women punch me; more than one dude drew a gun on me: and before long, I'd hired a bouncer to act as my body guard.

I was newly married and quickly building a reputation as the biggest jerk in town. Everyone knew who I was, but nobody wanted to be me. I was out until 3 AM, six nights a week, drunk every night, avoiding my family and about to be divorced if something didn't change. So, I quit, but that wasn't enough.

Small, West Texas towns, are a hard place to change. Sure, you might have forgotten about the jerk you used to be, but nobody else wants to. Finally, we had to leave town to escape my reputation. It was the only way I could resist the temptation to go back. Everyone already hated me, but the money was good, and the lure of being a local celebrity was a powerful drug to me.

So, from West Texas, the prodigal came home to Tulsa, looking for a way to be famous. I'd tried music, television, magazines, and comedy, but the one industry I hadn't tried yet, was professional athletics. So, I suited up and went to try out as the on-field personality for the Tulsa Drillers, a minor league baseball team.

I immediately began to look for a way to work myself up the ladder, but, they didn't need a rockstar, it seemed, and I got fired quickly.

Nothing was working, it seemed, so I went back where I'd started. Rock and Roll had at least wanted me.

I decided to take my music seriously. I started writing my own music and touring this time, with my own show. But, just as in the past, about the time we started to show promise, the band fell apart.

You would think by now I'd be ready to give in, but I had one more idea, the ultimate reality TV show.

I was on my way to pitch the concept when God spoke up again. "You know, I've still got a plan for your life, Kelly."

It ticked me off. If He'd wanted to help me, I'd given Him plenty of opportunities. Besides, I'd already tried the ministry thing when I was thirteen, and then again at eighteen, giving up my college scholarship. I wasn't about to change everything just to see it all fall apart, so I made God a deal.

"Every time I've tried to be a minister, it's ended badly. That's just not my thing. So, I'll open my heart to you, but you have to make the changes, I'm not making any promises, and I'm not changing a thing, just to end up back where I started."

Within a day, my thinking changed. The first thing I noticed was my desire to go to church. We'd started and stopped so many times it just seemed ridiculous to even try anymore. But, there was nothing I wanted more than to be there.

I can't explain it. It wasn't in me, then it was. So, rather than drag my family through it again, I went by myself.

As I started moving closer to Jesus, I noticed He was changing my attitudes from the inside out. Finally, I came to the point that I knew I would have to deal with the preaching thing again, so I started sending out emails to churches to get a youth pastor job, the only thing I felt qualified for.

Not one single reply.

But, I knew I needed to preach, it was so deep in me, that I got depressed over not getting any response.

"I know you told me to preach and travel, but no one wants me. What can I do, if no one will let me preach?"

The messages I'd sent had all been accompanied by my picture. I wanted to be honest about who I was. What good would it do to get them to invite me, then when I show up, show me to the door because of my tattoos and piercings, and the fact that I didn't look like any pastor I'd ever met. So, I signed up for Bible college.

I knew God was calling me to preach, and if no one wanted me now, I would make sure I was ready when they did.

By this point, I was feeling a bit like my man David. Here he's been anointed king, but he keeps getting sent out to take care of the sheep. It was hard too, he had to fight off lions, and tigers, and bears, oh my! He was frustrated, so, when he got a chance to take some food to his brothers, who were camped with the army, listening to Goliath perform his daily set.

Seriously, as an insult comic, I never had anything on Goliath.

"Send down your toughest dude. I'll rip him into pieces small enough to feed to the ducks!" This dude was harsh!

But what David knew (that I didn't get yet), was that he was already prepared. If he could kill a lion and a bear, surely a giant was no big deal. So, he asked for a shot. But, they laughed at him. It got so bad, in fact, King Saul literally had his armor put on the kid, so he could laugh at him, trying to stand up under all of it, and his brothers were even worse.

They told him to go home, stop stirring up trouble. But, the more they harassed him, the more he wanted a shot at the giant.

I was starting to feel the same way. The more I studied and prayed, the stronger the desire to preach burned in me.

Finally, I asked God, "Look, you want me to preach, but no one will invite me, so what do I do? I'll do anything!"

"Start making videos," was the response I got.

Immediately, an image of me, sitting at my laptop, uploading my cheesy three-minute sermon video popped into my head. Inside, my retired, insult-comic-self was already making fun of my new preacher self, and I could read the comments.

It was awful.

There was no way I was putting my face out there like that. Once it was launched, the cat was out of the bag. I'd be accountable, and open to critique. No thanks.

So, I started a blog, instead. Nobody read it. I mean, nobody. I'd sit, waiting for comments. In my head, I heard the wind whistling, as tumbleweeds rolled across my screen. My blog was a ghost town of one, me.

"Why isn't this working, God? I'm preaching, but no one is listening. I thought you called me..."

"To make videos," I heard His reply.

"Not start a blog."

Mad Max. Not joking, my first video was on Mad Max and how Satan is more subtle than an apocalypse thriller. You don't see him coming, and before you know it, you end up where you shouldn't be. It was special. All 97 viewers confirmed it. But for me, it was as if my dreams had been fulfilled! Those 97 people, somehow, met a need that touring across country, playing to sold out bars, producing my own television show and publishing a magazine couldn't touch.

I was home. Finally, I was getting a chance to preach! People were listening. They were being touched and sharing my message.

So, I made more videos, and it started to grow. I started to get emails from viewers, and the audience was growing, from 90 to 100 to 1000. Finally, one of my videos broke out!

I remember how excited I was as I watched it rocket up to 50,000 views! But so far, I was still just working in a cell phone shop, and going to Bible College. This isn't what I'd imagined, but I kept going.

Then, I made "Is it a Sin to Get a Tattoo," and overnight, things changed.

In a week, the video had been watched over two million times. People were commenting, sharing and debating my work. I got emails, phone calls, plane tickets, speaking requests. It was like heaven opened.

At that moment, God pulled back the curtain and showed me that what I thought was a desire for fame, was really a dream about being fulfilled and it was coming true. But, the kicker was, way back in the beginning, the thing that had slammed all of those doors in my face, my less than professional appearance, was kicking them open faster than I could answer the messages.

God had used what the world had used as a disqualification, to qualify me, big time.

"You're a shepherd!"

"Go home, who's watching the sheep?"

"Does dad know you're here?"

The voices just went right over David's head. He was too busy looking along the brook for the perfect stones. The slingshot skills he'd perfected as a shepherd was his weapon. If it were me, I'd have been looking around for an M16, or a grenade, not a slingshot.

But David had to use what God had given him. He knew he could do it. If God trusted him enough to be king, surely God would help him now.

When David stepped onto the field, he gave Goliath the perfect response, "You come out here with your military skills and your flashy weapons, and your big mouth, but I've got God on my side. I'm not going to rip you to shreds. Instead,

I'm going to kill you, then take your sword and cut off your head."

And the giant laughed, while David was splitting his skull with a rock and the last sight his big eyes saw, was tiny little David standing over him, with his own sword, as it came down, and his head rolled away from his body.

Me? I ended up quitting my job and going into full-time ministry. In the year after that video went viral, I've had more public attention than I can keep up with.

I've done radio interviews; TBN invited me out to do a segment. I've preached in 35 different states and two foreign countries. I was invited to be a speaker in the only traveling youth conference currently in existence. My WHY cards are in all 50 states, five foreign countries, and we've sent out over 40,000 of them. But, none of this is about me.

Just like David, I see people hurting, crushed under the giant heel of the world's system and, like David, I'm called to slay that giant by showing them a better way. I've got to use the weapons at my disposal. My ministry can't be yours or anyone else's. So, I tell jokes, stand in front of crowds and make a fool of myself, tell stories, share Scripture and hope that at least one of my stones finds its target each time.

How about it, want to come throw some rocks with me?

CHAPTER 15
"I've Been Broke, Out Of Love, But I Know, We're Not Alone"
-The Mowgli's

When we set out to engage in the Reckless Love Revolution, we don't get to put demands on God, or the people we work with. In fact, just like Legion, the woman at the well, and the Eunuch, we need to be prepared to partner with whoever shows up. We never know who God will send. He's used some very unlikely messengers to share his messages, from angels to pagan kings. No one is disqualified from God's mission. God holds open auditions, and he uses everyone who's willing to take part.

Sometimes, this is awesome, right from the beginning, everything just works. Other times, it takes some patience on our part, and the willingness to trust God that

He knows what He's doing. Even when our ministry partners seemingly fail us, He knows where we are. He sees the beginning from the end.

David and I both started out alone. Later, we find that David becomes an awesome warrior, like a certified rockstar. He ran around with Saul's son, Jonathan, another hardened warrior and they formed a band of men, known as David's

Mighty Men. They were legendary. But, had David not stepped out and followed God to kill Goliath, none of this would have ever happened.

I knew that the vision God had given me was way too big for one guy. I could barely keep up with just the beginning of what God was doing, and I knew it was going to grow. But, who would I take with me? I had no clue. I knew I needed someone that would share my vision and help me stay on track. We'd be on the road a lot and staying true to my wife, and kids was important. Plus, he had to be cool.

As I studied Jesus' ministry, I saw that He liked to pair people up in twos. I wanted a partner, and God had my back. Through the years, I've heard several speakers that just get me, and whenever they show up, I want to be there. But at the top of my list, was Judah Smith. I found out he was going to be speaking in Tulsa and I was determined to get a seat. So, I showed up three hours early, like a fan boy, to get a good seat.

I just knew I was going to walk up and be the first guy in line, but there was this skinny guy, who had to be crazy. After all, who else comes to church three hours early?

If you've ever met me, you know I can start a conversation with a fence post, so we started talking. He told me about his work as a school teacher. I love kids. He shared his vision to become a preacher. I was already on my way to do just that.

But, it wasn't just that he wanted to preach, the message on his heart was nearly identical to what I'd been sharing.

At that moment, it was like God tapped me on the shoulder, "You've been wanting a partner. You're welcome."

I knew that I would be seeing him again soon, so I suggested we trade numbers, "just in case," I wanted to play it cool.

Inside, my inner kid was doing cartwheels. I needed to remember this guy; this was a God appointment, I just knew it. When the doors opened, we parted ways, and I didn't want to put too much pressure on the guy. But, once I found my seat, I looked around and located Ryan. I needed to remember, so I took out my phone and, without being too obvious, I snapped a picture of this guy.

Creepy, right? It gets worse. It's still the icon on my phone! I was convinced, like love at first sight, that he and I were going to change the world together.
The thing is, it made no sense. He's tall and thin. I'm square. We don't have the same style. I'm a musician. He's a jock. He's a school teacher. I'd be stopped for questioning just walking up to most schools. It was not, from a human viewpoint, exactly a match made in heaven. But, something told me that this was more than a chance meeting.

Over the next year, we texted each other a few times. We had enough in common that a casual friendship emerged. Then one night in a Bible College lecture, God told me to read a passage. So, I did, and as I took it in, He laid out a plan.

"The next time you get invited to speak at an FCA event, you need to share this passage." Which was weird, because I'd never spoken to an FCA group before. I kind of wondered if I was just adding details to something, but I wrote it down anyway.

The very next day, I got a phone call. It was Ryan. Up until then, we'd only exchanged texts, so I wondered what it could be about. Turns out, Ryan had been invited by his church to be the guest speaker at an FCA event. But, for some reason, he offered me the gig.

At the time, I didn't know that Ryan had wanted that gig himself, but felt like God wanted him to give it to me.
 In fact, God had told him that if he gave up this opportunity for me to speak, I would give something to him. Six months later, that came about.

God shared the idea for Reckless Love Revolution with me. But, at first, I was selfish. I didn't want to share. I'd waited a long time, been through hell, skidded down on a highway on my own flesh to get to this point and I didn't want to share the spotlight.

God knows me so well. Immediately after the vision became clear, He told me to share it with Ryan. That he was the partner I needed and would be my co-founder. My desire to be obedient overruled my selfishness, and I called him and shared what God had shown me.

"Half of this is yours, what are we supposed to do with this?"

There was silence on the other end. "Hello?"

That's when Ryan shared his half of the story; how God had shown him that I would be bringing something to him if he would make the sacrifice of giving up his speaking slot for the FCA rally.

It was like the clouds parted and angels were singing. We couldn't have been surer of what we were doing. God had fit it together so perfectly.

We still had no idea where we would start. Then, I got a call.

A new youth conference had space open up. They needed someone to do random acts of kindness with 400 kids on the last day of the conference. Could I help out?

It was a perfect opportunity. My heart was leaping out of my chest, then they said, "We can't pay you, we will offer you this spot, and cover your travel, but you have to cover your expenses."

I didn't care. This was what I'd been looking for my whole life. A chance to preach like this was perfect! I called Ryan, and we started promoting.

Then the other shoe dropped. Two weeks out from the conference, I got a call. It seemed that things had changed. They still had a slot for us, but couldn't even pay our travel expenses. I was devastated. I was still in school, barely making any money. It might as well have been a million dollars. What was I going to do?

I had to call Ryan and let him know. I felt like I had failed. I'd failed God, somehow, and I'd failed Ryan. And the people who were excited about what we were doing. It was a disaster. So, I made the call.

"Okay, no problem," Ryan said.

It was not the response I expected. He was a school teacher. He couldn't make much more than I did at the phone store, why was he so calm about it.

"Well, I have a little side business I haven't told you about yet. And, as part of that, I can pay for my ticket on a company credit card. Plus, I have it setup so that every ticket I buy, gets a buddy pass that will cover your flight."

Instantly, I felt silly. Of course, God had worked this out way before I even knew about the conference. Of course, He'd prepared my ministry partner to supply this need.

Why had I felt so overwhelmed? Just days before, I'd been so excited and this one little bump in the road, after everything, had been almost enough to throw me off. It was a widow's oil jar story, and I just simply didn't have the faith to see beyond the moment.

That's what happens when we have preconceived ideas of how things should work.

Ryan and I could not have started this thing without each other. He needed my connections, and I needed his buddy pass. God saw the needs way before I did. If I had dismissed Ryan or told the conference, no thanks, we might never have gotten off the ground.

When we prejudge because they don't look like what we'd choose for a best friend. Or things appear to be falling apart, so we miss out. Our obedience is key to this.

You can't have a preconception in your mind of the perfect candidate in your church. You may be overlooking exactly what you need. It might be right in front of you. We are looking for a perfect fit, we need a perfect worship leader with the right look and feel, but the outcome could be even greater if we don't develop those relationships God puts in front of us we miss out. Had I looked for a partner, he would like the same music and movies. We would be totally compatible. But, my ideas suck. God's ideas sound stupid to me, but they work.

Sometimes we need to find what feels completely ridiculous because it works. God used a donkey to save a prophet from an angel with a flaming sword, had a prophet stage a theatrical performance to warn Israel of a coming siege, and had a rich man dip himself in a muddy river to cure his disease. And, in every case, there's a reason. It all fits.

In fact, I have to laugh when people use "logic" as an argument against God. Because, frankly, He's not that into fitting into our human logical constructs. He invented thinking "outside the box." We are so limited in our imagination, and all He sees are possibilities. So, the next time God hands you an opportunity, and a bump in the road comes along, just remember, God knows.

CHAPTER 16
"Love Is A Many Splendored Thing"
- Moulin Rouge

One of my favorite Hollywood movies of all time has got to be "Moulin Rouge." It's an epic love story of nearly biblical proportions, about a man willing to sacrifice himself to redeem a woman that can never be the life partner he wants. It's funny, it's sad, and it's very moving. But, at the center of this film is an idea that I think is flipped on its head wrong.

"The greatest love, you'll ever know... is to love, and be loved in return..."

This haunting melody echoes through my memory every time I watch this movie, and it's a powerful message. Love returned is an amazing experience, no doubt, but for my money, there is a greater love.

It's the love we experience with our Creator. To me, the line should be flipped around.

"The greatest love, you'll ever know, is to be loved, and love in return."

It's all we can do. We can never initiate the Reckless Love Revolution. It's too late. It was begun the moment He said, "Let there be light."

This epic love story we've been talking about is the central thread of all of history from the beginning, to right now and carrying on until the end of the age.

We love because He first loved us.

That's what we're calling you to hear, and it's no easy thing.

You see, that means you don't get to choose your targets.

That means it's not about you. That means you can't set your expectations on returns here. It's all about Him, His love for us, and His glory when we continue that love to others.

So, now we find ourselves here, on the launching pad. But, I wouldn't be doing you any favors, if I didn't provide a bit of a warning. Up to now, I've been presenting this as an optional thing for Jesus followers, and that's true to a point. But, what we haven't talked much about is, what happens when you opt out?

It's kind of funny how we talk about love in our world. We say you "fall in and out of love" like it's a big hole in the ground or something, and I can get behind that. I mean, I've seen people fall into a hole. It's funny. I know I shouldn't, but if I see you fall in a hole, I'm going to laugh. I'll help you out, but the first thing that's going to happen is me laughing.

But, here's something weird to think about: have you ever seen anyone fall out of a hole? How does that work? Reverse gravity? I don't know. And I'm pretty sure love doesn't work that way either. We choose to love, or we choose not to love. But when it comes to Jesus love, once you've chosen it, there's not much way to choose your way out.

I suppose you could fight your way out. He's not into forcing people, but why? Once you've experienced, you're going to want to share it. So, for those that don't, I feel like I should really say a few words about what you're going to experience.

See, love is like water. Yeah, you've probably heard some love metaphors, before, but not like this one. Just keep reading.

Water has to circulate. It comes from a source, travels, evaporates, and comes around again. But, what happens when it doesn't?

It's kind of like my grandma. When I was a kid, I spent a lot of time at Grandma's house, and I loved it. Well, most of it. My grandma, like a lot of Grandma's, had this thing about being thrifty. But, she took it to extremes. I don't know if it was stories about the Great Depression, or what, but she got it in her head that the world was a scarce place. Not just the world, but her world specifically.

Ironically, she also wanted to be a generous person, which led to some interesting shopping sprees. We'd go to the store, and Grandma always carried her Polaroid camera. Every time I'd see something I liked, she'd snap a picture of it. Like a shirt? Here, hold that up, snap! Like that toy? Okay, snap! Then she'd take these images home, but we'd never buy anything. Weird, right? It gets weirder.

From those photos, the next time I came over, she would create these elaborate gifts. She'd make that shirt...or al-most. Or that toy, and give it to me. It was kind of great. I got to thinking my Grandma could make almost anything. It was pretty cool until I was at school and got made fun of for wearing a "Nikey" shirt.

One year, I'll never forget it, the toy to own for Christmas, was a "My Buddy" doll. They'd show it in the commercial climbing up a tree with the kid, or riding bikes, and they were best friends. I just had to have one. So, I told Grandma, and sure enough, she made me my own "My Duddy" doll. It looked just like it. I took that thing everywhere, until one night, I fell asleep at Grandma's.

About the same time My Buddy came out, another little boy doll became famous in a horror movie, Chucky. Well, my un-cle thought it would be hilarious to show this movie to a little kid, and I fell asleep, dreaming of its evil little face, "My Dud-dy" curled up beside me.

Sometime in the middle of the night, I woke up, with Duddy's hands around my throat, screaming!
My uncle was using my own doll to choke me out! He thought it was hilarious, but for me, that was the end of Grandma's knockoffs.

So, why did I tell you that? Let me take you on a little tour of the Holy Land to explain. In the Bible, there are a lot of fa-mous bodies of water. Two of the most memorable are The Dead Sea that Israel crossed over in a scene made famous by Charlton Heston in the Ten Commandments on their way out of Egypt. And the Jordan River that they crossed over at the end of their journey to enter Canaan.

Like I was saying earlier, water can be life giving, or stagnant and nothing represents it better than these two rivers. The Jordan runs through fertile farm land. The water comes in, and the water goes out, a healthy river that's used for live-stock, and even human consumption. But, at the end of the river, lies the Dead Sea. Water goes in; nothing comes out. Famously, nothing lives in the Dead Sea, thus its name.

This is an important principle for us in life. We must have give and take. Ebb and flow. Receiving and giving out. If we don't, we end up stagnant, like my Grandmother.

Wow, that's kind of a harsh thing to say about my Grandma, isn't it? It would be, except, she didn't have to live like that.

Contrary to her belief, the world is an abundant place, with more than enough to go around. The thing was, she had more than enough. In fact, I wouldn't say she was Trump rich, but the cost of a Nike shirt or two and a My Buddy doll wouldn't have been missed at all. She died with more than many will ever see, living her life in fear of not having enough, while she had plenty.

She was like the Dead Sea, and that refusal to allow money to flow through her life made her fearful and robbed her of many great experiences. So, what's the lesson here?

For those of us who've experienced the love of Jesus, we have more than enough flowing into our lives. It's up to us. Will we be like the River Jordan, allowing the love and every-thing it brings with it, to flow through us to others, enriching the lives around us, and creating a happy, healthy harmony? Or, will we build a dam and horde it, trying to hold on in fear that there won't be enough?

I can tell you from experience; you want to be in the flow. Stagnation is no fun. It breeds death and disease. When we give and receive with open hands, however, we become a conduit for God to pour His blessing through.

As we give out, we make room for more, and the supply is never-ending.

So, as you think through what we've shared and you dream about what comes next. Don't just sit on it. You'll stagnate, and that's never good. First, you'll poison yourself with fear and bitterness. Then, you'll begin to infect the lives around you, and present a bad reflection of the Reckless Love Revolution He came to begin in you.

As you get out and start to practice loving people when it doesn't make sense, finding the value in everyone, and being open to interruption, you're going to find that you receive much more than you give.

Not only that, but as you increase your giving, the inflow seems to increase as well. But, if you take this love for granted and don't share it, don't keep pouring it out, the flow can stop.

Why? Because Jesus loves you very much, but just like I love all my kids and won't let them abuse each other, He won't let you minister in a way that's destructive either. You can do it, but you'll have to do it under your own power, and it's hard, and it's not much fun.

See, when we stop allowing the flow, and we begin to gather resources for our own uses, we get calcified. Then we begin to build programs and systems, where random acts of kindness, and reckless love used to be. And as this happens, much like the men at Babel, we begin to look to our "model" to do the work for us, and that's dangerous.

We can't be married to our programs. We need to be married to obedience. When we romanticize programs, they become idols. When this happens to me, God generally asks, "Did you move onto the next thing?"

If not that's where you're stuck. He may be asking you to give up everything you've built. But, if it's not of Him, He can't use it in the miraculous, God-breathed ways we've been talking about. It will be the same, wheezing, just barely shuffling forward religion the world is shying away from.

When you're in the flow, you'll know. Structures come and go, but if God is building them, they go up quick, and letting go is easy. If you've had to work to get it, you'll have to work to keep it. There's always provision with calling.

Just like Moses had to tell the children of Israel to stop giving when they brought more than was needed for the Tabernacle. But, if it's all you can do to keep going, maybe it's time to let go. God's calling you to something new.

As we stay in the flow, The Word never changes, but even within Scripture, the method was never the same. Don't change your love, don't change Jesus, but hold onto what you build for Him loosely.

Otherwise, we start to stagnate, and things begin to atrophy and die.

Some churches may say, "you don't know us, or what we've gone through."

What I do know is that we can control our own reactions to everything, which gives us a different outcome. It's how you react to those events. If your reaction is to trust, you're on top of the outcome, instead of it being on top of you.

When my grandmother died, she didn't just leave behind enough for a few shirts. There was an awesome inheritance, left to my mom and her brother. More than enough to have had an incredible life, but she was living in fear and hoarding, and we can be just like that with the things God shows us.

So, here is a personal challenge to the reader of this book. What will you do with what you've learned here? Will you hold on and stagnate, or begin a flow? It can be just you. Just you. Yes, it's going to shake things and change things, but the greatest impact is in you. That impact in you is going to be noticeable, perhaps your "Why" campaign starts within your church.

We've been talking about the great commission, which is telling us to go, but in Matthew 10, He says, "Start in your city, the same people out there are in your church and home too."

It doesn't have to be big and dramatic. It might just be a trickle in the beginning. But start that flow. Remind those who already know Him what it's all about. The key we've been saying is to go out and do this, but it has to start in your house. In your church. In your job.

Don't forget, the power of one can change this. You have to be a part of it. Don't hide it.
A revolution involves many, but it always starts with ONE.

Jesus said, "If a home owner owns a candle stand, he doesn't hide his candle under a basket, where no one gets the benefit. Instead, he puts it in a candle stand, so that the whole house can benefit from the light it gives."

This same fire, I'm warning you, if you let it stagnate, will consume you, just as Ezekiel said, "The word of God was like a fire in his bones."

Now that you know, you're responsible, don't let others unwillingness to catch the vision slow you down or intimidate you. This is not about them, or you. It's about Jesus.

As you get out and begin to experience some of these same things that we've already been practicing, we want to hear about it. Your neighbors want to hear about. People in neighboring towns want to hear about it. The world needs good news, and the good news we've got is the best news there is. So share it with us.

As I put this book to bed and move on to what's next, let me encourage you; go after a life of love as if your life depended on it. Because it does.

ABOUT THE AUTHOR

Kelly K is a Husband, Father of five, Preacher, Teacher, Writer and Motivational Speaker. Preaching the love of Jesus in a manner that is both progressive and passionate. Kelly K is a highly sought-after conference speaker, and social media Evangelism teacher. His messages reach out to inspire and encourage millions of lives through many multimedia platforms.

Kelly K's approach to speaking focuses on bridging the gap of cultures, ages, and society by offering a sound that is relative to every listener. His message is one of love, faith, joy and hope in Jesus Christ. Kelly K travels to any distance to share this amazing reckless love of Jesus and offer a new perspective on how to reach a world that is used to tuning out anything even slightly, "religious". So many have been blessed by the words, love and passion of Kelly K.

Kelly K currently lives in Kingfisher, Oklahoma with his beautiful wife Lindsay, and his five children, Brennen, Chase, Avery, Jaxx, and Jett. He is currently the Associate Pastor at Limitless Church of Kingfisher

CONNECT WITH ME

FOLLOW KELLY K ON SOCIAL MEDIA FOR DAILY POSTS,

VIDEOS, SERMONS, BIBLE STUDIES, AND MORE!

 @KellyKMinistries

 Facebook.com/TheKellyK

 @KellyK_13

 YouTube.com/KellyKMinistry

www.KellyKMinstries.com

TO REQUEST KELLY K TO COME AND SPEAK AT YOUR CHURCH OR

EVENT, PLEASE EMAIL:

KELLYKOPP@GMAIL.COM

This ministry is completely funded through the generosity of people like you! Thank

you for sowing into what God is doing through Kelly K Ministries.

 @KELLYK13 $KELLYKOPP13

Made in the USA
Columbia, SC
05 November 2024

45476605R00130